Randi Hill can still re... other teenage girl. Her life wasn't that unusual, but she had what she considered to be a lively social life. That was before Max, the lovable but lunatic alien, descended from her far-off planet and moved in with the Hill family to learn about being human. Max is logical, quite peculiar looking and amazingly quick to learn. In a funny, haphazard way she fits in with Randi and her friends.

Until one day she calmly announces she wants to learn about love. Randi has a boyfriend, Gary, so why can't Max just choose the man of her dreams and fall in love too? Randi is very uneasy at this romantic masterplan, and she senses disaster around the corner when Max announces her chosen partner – sultry Chad Bellamy, leader of the local rock band, a well-known heartbreaker and boyfriend of their arch-enemy, Desiree!

ANOTHER BOOK BY MARILYN KAYE

# MAX ON EARTH

# MAX IN LOVE

### MARILYN KAYE

PUFFIN BOOKS

Puffin Books, Penguin Books Ltd, Harmondsworth, Middlesex, England
Viking Penguin Inc., 40 West 23rd Street, New York, New York 10010, U.S.A.
Penguin Books Australia Ltd, Ringwood, Victoria, Australia
Penguin Books Canada Ltd, 2801 John Street, Markham, Ontario, Canada L3R 1B4
Penguin Books (N.Z.) Ltd, 182–190 Wairau Road, Auckland 10, New Zealand

First published in the U.S.A. by Pocket Books, a division of
Simon & Schuster, Inc. 1986
Published in Puffin Books 1987

Printed and bound in Great Britain by
Cox & Wyman Ltd, Reading
Typeset in Times

For my father and stepmother,
Harold and Meli Kaye,
with love

# Chapter One

"Well, what do you think?"

The thin, pale girl with short, golden hair stood stiffly before Randi Hill and Ellen Brent in Randi's bedroom. Shopping bags and crumpled tissue paper littered the floor.

"Max picked this outfit out all by herself," Ellen said, sounding like a mother whose child had just learned something new. Both girls were looking at Randi eagerly, waiting for some sign of approval.

Randi eyed the outfit critically. Max's taste was certainly different from her own, but she had to admit the girl was definitely developing a personal style. The pale yellow oversize shirt softened her boyish figure, and the wide straw belt emphasized her tiny waist. A short olive-green skirt revealed long, thin legs, and the peculiar laced-up sandals that reached halfway up her legs gave the whole getup a punk look.

Max was beginning to look anxious. "Do you not like this?"

"It's—interesting," Randi said finally. Then, noting the slightly dismayed look on Max's face, she quickly added, "It suits you. I mean, it's not something *I'd* wear, but then—I'm not you." Suddenly an image passed through her mind of that wretched one-piece black thing that Max had been wearing when Randi first found her. *This* was a definite improvement, and she tried to sound more enthusiastic. "I like it, Max, really I do. You look like something out of a fashion magazine."

Max brightened and turned to examine herself in a mirror.

"I just love human clothes," she said with a happy sigh.

"And they look very nice on you," Ellen said approvingly. "I only wish I could wear really trendy clothes like that," she added, mournfully contemplating her own rather chunky figure.

"You made a very nice selection," Randi said, and then almost laughed as she realized how she and Ellen were both talking to Max as if she were a child. But in a funny way, she *was*—after all, she'd only been on this planet for four weeks.

As Max and Ellen pored through the bags and discussed their purchases, Randi let her thoughts wander back to that amazing day when Max first arrived on Earth. Sitting on the bleachers, watching Randi and the other Riverside High cheerleaders go through their routines, Max had been a strange sight with her pale golden hair and black clothes. Randi had thought she was a runaway, and brought her home. A shiver ran through her as she recalled that moment when Max finally revealed to her that she was from another planet, that she had beamed herself down to Earth in the hopes that she would find a better world here.

Randi shuddered mentally as she remembered how nervous Max had made her. Randi had been so fearful of what others would think if they knew her new friend was actually an alien. So far, she had managed to pass Max off as an amnesiac—a girl who had simply found herself one day sitting on the bleachers at Riverside High, who had no idea who she was or where she was from. Other than Randi, the only people who knew the truth about Max were her best friend, Ellen, and Randi's grandmother.

Still admiring herself in the mirror, Max said suddenly, "I must go show my new clothes to Gramma." She skipped from the room, and Ellen turned to Randi with an expression of wonderment.

"Amazing, isn't it? I mean, she's acting just like a normal person."

"After all, she *is* part human," Randi reminded her. "Her grandmother was a human being who got caught in a beaming experiment or something. But you're right—she has changed a lot in the past few weeks."

"Remember how she used to talk?" Ellen asked. "So stiff and formal—like a foreigner."

"That's because she *is* a foreigner," Randi noted dryly. "But she does talk normally now—sometimes. When she feels like it."

Ellen looked at her closely. "You've changed, too. You used to seem sort of embarrassed by her. Now you seem like you really like her."

Randi nodded. "I *do* like her. She's like a little sister to me—even though we're the same age. Anyway, I feel like I have to take care of her—you know, watch out for her."

Ellen agreed. "I know what you mean. I have to keep reminding myself that's she's still a stranger to our world. Like today at the mall—this real sleazy-looking guy called out to her, like he was trying to pick her up or something. And she was going to talk to him till I pulled her away!"

Randi grimaced. "That's what I mean—we've got to take care of her."

Ellen eyed her curiously. "How long do you think you're going to be able to pass her off as an amnesiac? What's going to happen when school starts?"

Randi closed her eyes. She'd been trying not to think about that. "I don't know," she admitted. "I guess I'll wait till my parents get home and see what they say." Her parents were archaeologists, and they'd been on a dig in Egypt all summer.

"When are they getting back?"

Randi frowned. "In two weeks. They were supposed to be back this week, but they found something important on that dig, so they have to stick around." Her frown deepened. "I wrote them that I have a friend staying here, but I don't think they're going to be prepared for Max. And I wonder if they're going to buy that amnesia story."

"Maybe you should tell them the truth about her," Ellen suggested. "After all, your grandmother seems to be handling it okay."

Randi had to laugh. "Gramma's the most open-minded person I know. I mean, she'll believe *anything*. Reincarnation, ESP, you name it. When I told her about Max, she wasn't even surprised. She said she'd always suspected there was life on other planets. Somehow I don't think my parents are going to be quite so open-minded."

"Why not?" Ellen asked. "They're real intellectual types. Once they hear Max's story, I'll bet they'd believe her. . . ."

"Maybe so," Randi said, "but that might even be worse. They'd want to analyze her culture, study her like a scientific curiosity. They'd drag her off to conferences and show her off like some freak. I can't let that happen to Max."

Ellen was silent for a minute. "I guess you're right," she said finally. "You know, it's funny, Randi. We've known each other all our lives. But I hardly know your parents at all."

Randi laughed shortly. "Neither do I." Ellen looked puzzled, and Randi explained. "They're hardly ever around. As long as I can remember, it's been me and Gramma, with my parents just showing up between digs."

Ellen looked so sympathetic that Randi hastened to reassure her. "It's okay, really," she said quickly. "I know that they love me. Gramma and I get along so well that I hardly even miss my parents at all."

5

That last part wasn't totally honest—she *did* miss her parents, and sometimes she wondered what it would be like to have a more normal family life, with parents who stayed at home. But she tried not to think about that too much.

The phone rang just then, and Randi grabbed it from the nightstand by her bed.

"Hello?"

"Hi, it's me."

The mere sound of Gary's voice sent a tingle through her.

"Hi, you."

"The movie starts at eight, so I'll pick you up at seven-thirty, okay?"

"Okay."

"See you then. Bye."

"Bye."

It wasn't much of a conversation, but it was enough to make Randi feel high as a kite. As she replaced the receiver she felt like she was on a cloud. She'd only been dating Gary Morrison for two weeks, but she'd been in love with him all summer.

"From the expression on your face, I gather that was Gary," Ellen said with a grin.

Randi smiled dreamily. "I still can't believe I'm actually going out with him. We're a real couple now, and sometimes I have to pinch myself to believe it."

Ellen cocked her head to one side and looked at Randi quizzically. "Have you told him about Max?"

"Huh?"

6

"Does he know that Max is from another planet?"

Randi shook her head firmly. "No. I don't think Gary's ready for something like that."

"You know, it's kinda funny," Ellen mused. "If it hadn't been for Max, you and Gary might never have gotten together."

Randi bristled a bit at this. "Well, *eventually* he probably would have noticed me on his own," she said, faking a confidence she really didn't feel. "But Max certainly speeded up the process!"

Ellen giggled. "I wish I could have been there that night at Gino's when Gary caught Desiree with Chad Bellamy. How did Max arrange that, anyway?"

Randi rolled her eyes as she recalled that bizarre night. "Max knew that Gary and Desiree were going together. And she knew that I had a major crush on Gary. When she heard Desiree brag about how she was seeing Chad behind Gary's back and meeting him at that pizza joint, she figured this was a perfect way to get Gary and me together." She smiled slightly. "I was furious with her at the time. But I have to admit, her scheme worked!"

"Wow," Ellen breathed. "I would love to have seen that snotty Desiree Dupont caught in the act. I can just imagine her face when you guys walked in!"

Randi laughed. "It was something, all right. She looked like she wanted to sink into the ground." Then her smile faded. "I get a little queasy when I think about her, though. I'm still wondering if she's planning to get back at me for this."

Ellen nodded understandingly. "I'd be worried, too.

After all, you *did* break the number one rule of the Stars—never mess with another Star's boyfriend."

"But it was all Max's idea," Randi began, but was interrupted by a call from downstairs.

"Girls! C'mon down and join us for a snack!"

Randi and Ellen entered the kitchen just as Randi's grandmother was slicing a freshly baked carrot cake. Max was eyeing it cautiously.

"Don't worry, Max," Randi assured her. "There's nothing that ever moved in that cake." Max was a strict vegetarian; in her own world nothing that had ever been capable of feeling could be eaten.

Max looked relieved. "Good," she said happily. "It smells delicious."

"It sure does," Randi agreed, and gave her grandmother a spontaneous peck on the cheek. She was rewarded with a big smile from the slightly plump but pretty gray-haired woman.

"Well, sit down and have some while it's still warm," she said briskly. "Who wants milk?"

They all gathered around the kitchen table, and Ellen asked Mrs. Hill if she liked Max's new clothes.

"Totally awesome," Gramma replied brightly.

Randi groaned. "Gramma, *nobody* uses that expression anymore."

"Nevertheless," her grandmother replied calmly, "you know what I mean. I think Max looks—well, whatever you kids say now to mean 'terrific.' "

"*Terrific* will do quite nicely," Max said. "And I thank you." Carefully she placed napkins on her lap and tucked one under her chin. "It is lovely to be able

8

to dress as I please. Where I come from, there are no clothes like this. Everyone dresses alike, talks alike, acts alike."

"Sounds pretty awful," Ellen mumbled, her mouth full of carrot cake.

Max's brow wrinkled. *"Awe-ful* and *awe-some*. The words are highly similar. What is the distinction, please?"

Ellen grinned. *"Awful* means bad, *awesome* means good."

"But nobody says *awesome* anymore, right?" Gramma asked.

"That's true," Ellen replied, "but if they did, it would mean good."

Max shook her head mournfully. "This is all highly illogical. Similar words having opposite definitions. English is a remarkably peculiar language."

Randi bit her lower lip. She wished Max would talk normally all the time. When she wanted to, she could—but so often she'd slip back into that odd, foreign way of talking. But Randi didn't say anything. When Max first arrived, Randi had ordered her around and tried to make Max conform. This had made Max unhappy, and now Randi was determined to let the girl just be herself—even if it drove Randi straight up the wall.

"There is so much that is still strange to me here," Max was saying. "But there is so much that is awe—I mean, terrific."

"What do you like best here that you didn't have on your planet?" Ellen asked.

Max didn't even pause to ponder the question. "Romance," she said promptly. "Romance and love." Suddenly she jumped up from her seat and ran out of the room.

Ellen's mouth fell open and she looked at Randi. "Is Max in love?"

Randi was bewildered. "Not that *I* know of."

Max reappeared just then, clutching a paperback book in her hand. "I have been reading this book," she said, showing the cover.

"*Love's Sweet Temptation,*" Gramma read aloud. "Good heavens, Max, where did you find *that?*"

"I guess it's mine," Randi admitted, looking a little shamefaced. "Remember last summer, Ellen, when we were reading those silly romances all the time?"

Max's pale eyebrows shot up. "Do you think this is silly? At least, by reading this book, I am gaining some knowledge of love."

Randi shifted uneasily in her seat. "You know, Max, you can't always believe what you read. I mean, that book's pretty romantic . . ."

"Exactly!" Max said.

"And speaking of romance," Gramma said, rising from the table, "there won't be any in my life if I don't start getting ready for my date tonight."

"Are you going out with Officer Bronski again?" Randi asked. When her grandmother nodded, Randi whistled. "Wow, this is getting pretty heavy," she said teasingly.

"Don't be silly," Gramma said quickly, but she was blushing as she left the room. She had been going out with the burly police officer for over a month, and she still got a certain expression on her face whenever his name was mentioned.

"Ellen, what are you up to tonight?" Randi asked. "Have you got a date?"

Ellen yawned. "Not really. I'm going to the video arcade with Bubba. I don't think you can actually call that a date."

Randi nodded as she envisioned Bubba Weintraub, her good-natured next-door neighbor who was everybody's pal. For a while he had had a big crush on Max, and they had dated a few times.

"And I'm going out with Gary," Randi said thoughtfully, and then turned to Max with a worried look. "That's going to leave you home alone, Max."

"You could come to the arcade with me and Bubba," Ellen suggested. "Like I said, it's not a real date."

"No, no," Max said quickly. "I thank you for your concern, but I prefer to stay home with my book."

Randi was puzzled. "Max, why haven't you finished that book by now? With your superior intelligence, you could zip right through it. Why, I've seen you read a book twice as thick in ten minutes!" And she knew that was no exaggeration. The intellect of Max's species was far above that of humans.

"Oh, yes, I have read it three times," Max replied placidly. "But now I am attempting to read it as a human would. Slowly, so that I can thoroughly appreciate it."

"Oh, I see," Randi said doubtfully. Somehow,

*Love's Sweet Temptation* didn't seem like the kind of book that one had to read slowly to appreciate.

"Well, I guess I'd better get going," Ellen said, pushing herself away from the table while wistfully noting a remaining slice of cake on the platter. "Even if it's just Bubba, I guess I ought to take a shower and change my clothes."

After she left, Randi got up to clear the table. "I guess I'd better start getting ready, too," she said as she piled the dishes in the sink. "Max, are you sure you don't mind staying alone tonight? You could go to the movies with me and Gary."

Max didn't respond. She was totally engrossed in her book.

"Max?"

She looked up then, but her expression was sort of dazed.

"Yes?"

"Would you like to go to the movies with Gary and me?"

"No, thank you," Max said politely, and returned to her book.

Randi shrugged and went upstairs to take a shower. When she returned to her room, Max was sitting at the vanity table, staring at herself in the mirror. *Love's Sweet Temptation* lay opened on the table. She seemed totally oblivious to Randi's presence, and Randi watched her curiously.

First, Max cocked her head to one side, and gazed at her reflection intently. Slowly her eyelids lowered, and a slight smile appeared. With her eyes half-closed, she then raised her eyebrows, so her face took on a dreamy, dazed expression—as if she'd just been hit on the head with a large heavy object and was suffering from a mild concussion.

"Max, what are you doing?"

The odd expression still intact, Max turned and faced Randi.

"What do I look like?" she asked.

Randi eyed her thoughtfully. "I'm not sure. What are you *trying* to look like?"

Max's face fell back to normal. "It isn't obvious?"

Randi shook her head. "Are you trying to look sick?" she asked helpfully.

Max scowled. "No." She returned to the mirror and again began rearranging her features.

Randi watched her in amusement as she began to dress.

"Max, why don't you tell me what you're trying to look like, and maybe I can help you."

Max examined her reflection for a moment and then turned to the book lying by her side. She studied a page and then looked in the mirror again. She turned her head to the left, then to the right. She widened her eyes, and then she narrowed them. She grinned broadly, showing all teeth, and then reduced it to a small smile. Finally she turned back to Randi.

"I'm trying to look like a woman in love."

Randi stared at her. "Who are you in love with?"

"No one," Max replied. "But I believe that if I

could at least *look* like I was in love, I could understand what it feels like."

Randi choked back an urge to laugh. "Max, it doesn't work that way. You have to *be* in love before you can look like you're in love. Besides, where'd you get the idea that people look a certain way when they're in love anyway?"

Max promptly picked up the paperback again and began reading aloud.

" 'She looked like a woman in love. Her eyes were deep, dark pools, holding secrets only one man could know. Her glistening lips held an open invitation, promising a delight never known before. Her skin glowed, with—' "

"Enough!" Randi screeched. "Max! You don't believe that garbage, do you? *Nobody* looks like that in real life."

Max frowned. "But it's right here, in print."

Before Randi could respond, the doorbell rang.

"Oh gosh, there's Gary now," she said, and reached for her pocketbook.

"That's it!" Max said suddenly. "That is how I want to look! You look just the way the girl in the book is described!"

Randi stared at her blankly. "Huh?"

Max beamed. "Look at yourself in the mirror. Think of Gary, and look at your face."

By now her grandmother had opened the door, and Randi could hear Gary's voice downstairs. She wanted to run down to see him . . .

"Look!" Max insisted.

Randi sighed, but obediently turned to look at herself in the mirror. Her hair looked nice, her lip gloss wasn't smeared—but she knew that wasn't what Max was referring to. It was her expression, the light in her eyes . . .

She had to admit that Max was right. This was definitely the look of a girl in love.

# Chapter Two

Randi was still thinking about Max as Gary parked the car at the mall.

"You're kind of quiet tonight," Gary said. "What's up?"

Randi sighed. "Nothing, really. I'm just a little worried about Max, that's all. I think I need to find her a boyfriend."

Gary turned to her quizzically. "What's the matter—can't she find her own?"

Randi shook her head. "It's not that easy. Max isn't like other girls, y'know? After all, how many other girls come from—" she almost choked on her words— "I mean, don't know where they come from? She needs someone special, someone . . . sensitive."

"You'd better be careful," Gary said as they walked through the parking lot. "Getting into the matchmaking business can be dangerous. You can kill a friendship that way."

"Oh, I'm not worried about that," Randi said confidently. "Max is like a sister to me. And I feel like I have to take care of her. She's—she's sort of gullible." She looked at Gary curiously. "Can *you* think of anyone for her? Maybe one of your friends?"

Gary shook his head decisively. "No way, Randi. I don't want to get involved."

Randi frowned. She'd hoped Gary would be more understanding. Even though he didn't know the real story about Max, surely he could see that she needed special attention. On the other hand, though, she knew that some people, especially guys, didn't like to fix people up. Things could get pretty awkward if the people didn't get along.

And she couldn't really be annoyed with him. Especially when he tossed his arm lightly around her shoulders, and she felt that wonderful, now-familiar tingle. Strolling through the mall, she basked in that marvelously comfortable feeling of having a boyfriend by her side. She didn't know what movie they were going to see, and she didn't really care. It was enough just to be with him.

But her heart sank a little when she saw the marquee on the theater. The title said it all: NIGHT OF HORRORS. And if that weren't enough, underneath the title were the words: YOU MAY NEVER HAVE A PEACEFUL NIGHT'S SLEEP AGAIN!

Randi shuddered. She hated scary movies. Gary must have read her expression, because he gave her a look of concern.

"What's wrong? Have you already seen it?"

"No," Randi said hesitantly, "it's just that . . . well,

I guess I'm not all that crazy about horror movies. All that blood and gore—sometimes I even have nightmares." She glanced at Gary apprehensively. Would he think she was being a baby?

But Gary just smiled understandingly. "Hey, that's okay. To tell you the truth, I'm not that crazy about these movies either. Let's see what's playing at the other theater."

Randi smiled and happily agreed. How lucky she was to have a guy like Gary! Another boy might have teased her about having nightmares—but not Gary.

The other theater was showing a romantic comedy that neither of them had seen. It was about a man and a woman who worked in the same office but never paid any attention to each other. Then they got involved in a zany mystery and ended up falling in love.

"I don't get it," Gary said as they walked through the lobby after the show. "I mean, how can a guy see a girl every day and ignore her and then suddenly fall in love with her?"

Randi grinned mischievously. "I'm not sure that's so unrealistic. After all, we used to see each other practically every day at school, and you never said much to me."

Gary blushed slightly. "You're right. Gosh, I must have been blind or something—"

"Well, *hello*."

The voice came from behind them, but Randi didn't need to turn around to identify that whine. When she *did* turn, it was reluctantly.

"Hi, Desiree."

As always, Desiree looked absolutely gorgeous. Her blond hair looked like spun gold, and her great figure was obvious in the tight cropped jeans and halter top she was wearing.

Randi didn't look at Gary, but she could visualize his expression. After all, he had gone out with Desiree for two months—and would probably still be going out with her if not for Max's scheming.

He muttered "hi" and then turned to Randi suddenly. "I think I left my jacket in the theater. I'll be right back." As she watched him walk rapidly back toward the theater, it was on the tip of Randi's tongue to say, "But you didn't wear a jacket"—and then she realized that he wanted to disappear.

She looked at Desiree nervously. This was the first time Randi had seen her since she started dating Gary. At least Desiree was smiling—if you could call that odd little smirk a smile.

"Have you and Gary been seeing a lot of each other?" she asked in a phony-sweet way. Wordlessly Randi nodded, and Desiree continued in that same tone: "How nice."

Randi couldn't tell if Desiree was being sarcastic or not. Uneasily she managed a half-smile.

"Well, uh, yeah," she said. "Since you guys broke up, I figured it was okay . . ." Her voice drifted off, and she wanted to kick herself. She knew she sounded as if she needed Desiree's permission to date Gary— which was ridiculous!

Desiree shrugged, as if the relationship was of absolutely no interest at all to her.

"Well, you can *have* him," she said disdainfully. "I only went out with him because there wasn't anyone *interesting* around. And jocks are such jerks, really. I was getting real tired of him."

That's not true, Randi thought indignantly. All jocks weren't jerks, and anyway, Gary wasn't actually a jock—he was only on the track team. But there was no point to getting into an argument with her, so she changed the subject.

"What are you up to this evening?"

Desiree casually examined her perfectly manicured long pink fingernails. "I'm meeting Chad at the Teen Scene. He's playing there tonight, you know."

Randi glanced over toward the other side of the mall, at the popular new dance club that had just opened. Sure enough, the sign outside proclaimed: NOW APPEARING—SPIT—RIVERSIDE'S HOTTEST BAND. "Oh yeah," she said, "Chad plays the guitar, right?"

"*Lead* guitar," Desiree replied pointedly. "And he sings some, too."

Randi nodded and tried to look suitably impressed. She didn't know Chad Bellamy at all, and she'd only seen him around a couple of times. He was older, eighteen at least, and terribly good-looking. She remembered once when Spit performed at a school dance, and all these girls couldn't take their eyes off him. Randi wasn't one of them, though. Personally, she thought he was too flashy-looking. Plus, there were rumors that he was pretty wild.

"By the way," Desiree said casually, "is that weird friend of yours still around?"

Randi pretended not to hear the word *weird*. "You mean Max? Sure, she's still around."

"Does she still have that—that *disease?*"

Randi rolled her eyes. "You mean her amnesia? It's not a disease, Desiree. It's—it's a condition, or something. I mean, you can't *catch* it."

Desiree shrugged. "Well, whatever it is, does she still have it?"

Randi nodded solemnly. "Yes, I'm afraid it . . . it may be permanent."

Desiree's eyes seemed to narrow, and Randi had a sinking suspicion that Desiree wasn't quite willing to accept that story.

"Do you mean she's going to be staying with you for *good?*"

"I don't know," Randi said honestly. "I'll have to wait and see what my parents think when they get back in two weeks." Knowing how Desiree felt about Max, she couldn't resist adding mischievously, "I think it might be fun having Max at Riverside High with us, don't you?"

Desiree glared at her. "No, I don't. And Randi, don't get any bright ideas about Max joining the Stars. She wouldn't fit in."

Even though Desiree's voice had a threatening edge to it, Randi was pleased to realize that she wasn't feeling as intimidated as she used to feel with Desiree.

"Oh, I wouldn't say that," she said nonchalantly. "I mean, the other girls seem to like her."

Desiree's eyes narrowed to the point where they were just tiny little slits. Randi knew from that expression that Desiree was about to say something particularly vicious, and it was with great relief that she saw Gary approaching.

"I guess I left my jacket in the car," he murmured, barely glancing at Desiree. Desiree raised her eyebrows and glanced pointedly at Randi, as if to say "See—I told you jocks were jerks." Randi ignored her expression and smiled brightly at Gary.

"I'm starving," she said. "How about you?"

Gary nodded. "Yeah, me, too. Let's get something to eat."

"And I'd better get over to the Teen Scene," Desiree said. "Chad just *hates* it if I'm not there when he's playing. I'll see you guys later." And she sauntered off toward the club.

Randi glanced at Gary's expressionless face, and she was pleased to note that his eyes weren't following her. Instead, he took Randi's hand and began walking purposefully toward El Muncho. He was quiet, though, and Randi felt a little uneasy. Had that encounter with Desiree upset him? Was he thinking about her? Was he—horror of horrors—*missing* her?

There was an empty booth in the restaurant, and without speaking they automatically headed there and sat down. Silently they accepted the menus from a waitress, and Randi pretended to study hers—while all the time wondering what Gary was thinking about. Finally he spoke.

"I think I'm going to have tacos. What about you?"

"I guess I'll have tacos, too," Randi replied. Actually, she didn't much like tacos. But then, she wasn't really very hungry anymore. She was too worried about what was on Gary's mind.

The waitress reappeared, and Gary gave her their order. Then he fell silent again. Randi summoned up her courage and caught his eye.

"A penny for your thoughts," she said lightly.

Gary smiled. "Is that all they're worth?"

Randi laughed nervously. "That depends . . ."

Gary's smile faded, and he looked thoughtful. "I was just thinking . . . about Desiree."

Randi felt sick. Two sodas appeared on their table, and she busied herself with taking the wrapper off her straw and stirring her drink. She didn't know what to say.

"It feels strange seeing her," he added.

Randi could feel tears forming in the back of her eyes. Was this it? Was he about to tell her that he wanted to get back together with Desiree?

Gary glanced around the restaurant. "We used to come here a lot."

Randi concentrated on her soda, which was beginning to look blurry.

"And I was just thinking," he continued, "how much nicer it is being here with you."

The sick feeling disappeared, and the tears in her eyes turned to stars.

"Oh, Gary," she said, sighing in relief, "you had me so worried."

He looked puzzled. "Huh?"

"I thought maybe seeing her had made you . . . want her back."

His eyebrows shot up, and his mouth fell open. "What? Are you kidding?"

The look of sincere astonishment on his face provided even more reassurance that her fears were needless.

"But you must have really liked her when you two were dating," she said.

"Look," Gary said, "I'll admit, when Desiree first asked me out, I was flattered."

"*She* asked *you* out?"

Gary grinned. "Yeah . . . anyway, she really came on to me. And I guess I didn't put up much of a fight. I mean, she's pretty good-looking, and all the other guys were telling me how lucky I was. But I was never happy with her. She was always whining about something, or complaining. She was never any fun."

Randi was bewildered. "But you two were dating for two months! If you were so miserable, how come you didn't break up with her?"

Gary looked embarrassed. "I guess I just didn't have the guts. I didn't want to hurt her feelings." He smiled. "That night Max dragged us into the pizza joint and Desiree was sitting there with Chad—boy, that was great. *Finally* I had an excuse to break up with her!"

Randi shook her head in amazement. All that time she had thought he was madly in love with Desiree! Guys were really strange. . . .

She was aware that Gary was looking at her intently.

"You know, Randi," he said hesitantly, "being with

you makes me feel so good. I think we have something special together."

Randi's heart was full. "Oh, Gary," she breathed, "I know what you mean. I feel the same way about you."

They looked deeply into each other's eyes. The tacos appeared just then, but they ignored them.

"I wish I had something to give you," he said suddenly. "I remember my dad telling me how, when he and my mom were in high school, he gave her his senior ring and she wore it on a chain around her neck. That meant that they were going steady and wouldn't date anyone else but each other."

"You don't have to give me anything," Randi said honestly. "I don't want to go out with anyone but you."

Gary's eyes were soft. "Randi . . ."

She smiled dreamily. "Yes?"

"I'm starving." He grabbed a taco and began munching it happily. Randi laughed.

"Me, too!" Funny, how quickly her appetite had returned! Was this what love did to you—make you hungry? If so, she'd better watch it, or she'd get fat in no time at all!

"By the way," Gary said in between mouthfuls, "my cousin Ralph's coming to town tomorrow. His family's moving to Riverside next month, and they're coming here this week to look at houses."

"Oh, yeah? What's he like?"

"I'm not sure," Gary said. "I haven't seen him

since we were little kids. He used to be really obnox-
ious and conceited. You know, the type who thinks he
knows everything. But he's probably changed since
then."

Randi had a sudden inspiration. "Why don't you
invite him to come out with us tomorrow night? We
could get him a date."

Gary shrugged unenthusiastically. "Yeah, I guess
we could. Though I'd rather we were alone. Besides,
who could we get him a date with?"

Randi grinned. "How about Max?"

Gary sighed, and then smiled. "Still planning on
being a matchmaker, huh? Better not get any big
ideas—he's only going to be here for a few days, and
then he won't be back in town for a month."

"I know, I know," Randi said, "but Max could use
the practice."

"Practice?"

"In dating," Randi said. "The only guy she's ever
been out with is Bubba. Besides, I think it's been kind
of lonely for her lately, with me out all the time."

Gary frowned slightly. "I just hope Ralph's not the
jerk he used to be. He was such a know-it-all."

"That's okay," Randi said confidently. "Max can
handle him. She's pretty smart herself, you know."
More than smart, she thought to herself. Of course,
Gary didn't know that Max came from a planet where
everyone had an intelligence much superior to people
on Earth.

"But if she can't remember anything, how do you
know she's so smart?" Gary asked.

Randi paused. A disturbing thought had just occurred to her. If she and Gary were going to be spending a lot of time together, wasn't it about time she told him the truth about Max? Would he understand? Would he think Max was crazy? Even worse—would he think Randi was crazy?

She brushed those thoughts aside. I'll deal with that later, she told herself.

"Just because Max has amnesia doesn't mean she's stupid," she said carefully. "I mean, it's true sometimes she doesn't understand things that we take for granted, and she asks odd questions. But she's basically intelligent—you know what I mean?" She wasn't sure she herself knew what she meant—but Gary just nodded.

"Yeah, okay, I guess it's better than just having Ralph tag along with us. I just hope you won't be too disappointed if Ralph turns out to be a total nerd, and he and Max hate each other."

"I won't be," Randi assured him. But in the back of her mind, she was thinking, wouldn't it be great if they really hit it off—and Max could learn what it's like to be in love.

She looked at Gary and smiled. She wanted Max to feel what *she* was feeling, right that minute.

# Chapter Three

*"It's a wonderful feeling,"* Randi sang as she popped slices of bread in the toaster, *"being in love, oh, yes, it's a wonderful feeling . . ."* She grabbed three plates from the cupboard and danced over to the kitchen table. *"And I'm in love, oh, yes, and I feel wonderful . . ."* Funny, she thought, I never liked that silly love song. But she continued humming it as she skipped around the table, placing the dishes on the mats.

Suddenly she was aware that Max was standing in the doorway, watching her.

"Good morning," she sang out.

Max didn't bother to return the greeting. "Why are you singing and dancing like that?"

Randi smiled happily. *"Because I'm in love,"* she warbled, *"oh, yes, and I feel wonderful."*

Max eyed her sternly. "But you have been in love for several weeks, and you haven't been singing and dancing."

Gramma caught those last words as she joined them in the kitchen. "Who's singing and dancing?"

Randi grinned as she reached into the refrigerator for eggs.

"*I* am," she said. "Gary and I had a very significant discussion last night."

Her grandmother looked intrigued. "And what was the nature of this significant discussion?"

"Well . . ." Randi paused dramatically before making her announcement. "We have an understanding. Like, we're not going to date other people. We have a *meaningful relationship*." As if to punctuate her announcement, the toast popped up at that moment. Randi pulled the slices out of the toaster, put them on a platter, and placed the dish on the table.

"How nice!" Gramma exclaimed. "Gary's such a lovely, sweet young man."

Randi winced at Gramma's old-fashioned description, but she appreciated her approval nonetheless. She turned to Max to see her reaction.

The pale alien was watching her carefully. "This means you are in love, is that correct?"

"You got it!"

"Very good," Max said approvingly. "I hope you will give me the benefit of this experience."

Now it was Randi's turn to look puzzled. "Huh?"

"You will explain to me the experience of love," Max said. "I find these literary explanations to be somewhat confusing. I need a more specific description. Please tell me what you are feeling at this moment."

29

Randi laughed. "I feel wonderful!"

Max shook her head impatiently. "That is an insufficient explanation. I am unable to relate to it."

Gramma smiled. "Well, *I* can relate to it. It's the way I feel about Carl Bronski. *We* have an understanding, too."

Randi gasped. "Gramma! Are you going to marry Officer Bronski?"

The older woman laughed. "No, no, nothing like that. This is the 1980s! A woman doesn't have to get married to have a meaningful relationship."

"I would like to have a meaningful relationship," Max said suddenly. "How do I get one?"

Gramma patted her hand affectionately. "Just let it happen, dear." She glanced at the clock. "Goodness, I'd better hurry or I'll be late for my meeting."

"Which meeting do you have today?" Randi asked.

Gramma looked momentarily uncertain. "I can't remember—I'd better check my schedule. But I *do* have a meeting, so if you girls will excuse me, I'll go get ready." She left the kitchen, and Max turned to Randi.

"How can I get one of these meaningful relationships?"

Randi grinned. "If I knew the answer to that, I would have been dating Gary a year ago!" And then she remembered something. "Look, Max, I can't promise you a meaningful relationship, but how would you like a blind date?"

"A blind date?"

"Gary's cousin Ralph is in town for the weekend.

30

Do you want to go out with him tonight? You'd be doubling with me and Gary. I don't know how you feel about blind dates, but . . ."

A definite spark of interest appeared on Max's face.

"A blind date! Yes, I would very much like to go. I am reading a very interesting book, *Love's Strange Fury*, in which the woman has a blind date and they fall madly in love. This could be an excellent opportunity."

"Now, hold on a minute!" Randi said hastily. "It's just a date . . ." She was interrupted by the phone ringing. She watched Max's enthusiastic expression anxiously as she grabbed the phone.

"Hello?"

"Hi, it's me." Gary's voice was so low, she could barely hear him. "Listen," he continued urgently, "I have to talk fast and I have to whisper. Have you asked Max about tonight?"

"Yeah," Randi replied, lowering her voice and glancing at Max, who had gone back to her book. "Why?"

"Well, you might want to talk her out of it," Gary whispered. "Ralph's just as big a creep as he was when we were kids. Maybe bigger."

Randi groaned. "Does he have to come along with us tonight?"

Gary echoed her groan. "Yep. My parents would kill me if I went out and didn't ask him along."

Randi was silent for a minute. "I better prepare Max," she said finally. "What are we going to do, anyway?"

31

"He wants to go to a video game arcade," Gary said mournfully. "He won some video game championship in his hometown, and I think he just wants to show off."

Randi sighed. She thought video games were boring, and she knew Gary wasn't very big on them either. And Max probably didn't have the faintest idea what video games were.

"Okay," she said in a resigned voice. "What time will you come for us?"

"I guess about eight," he said. "I'm not looking forward to this, Randi. I mean, this guy's really *weird*."

"Mmm." Randi shot a furtive look at Max. She didn't seem to be listening, but she whispered nonetheless. "Well, Max isn't the most normal person in the world either. Who knows? Maybe they'll hit it off."

"Maybe," Gary murmured, but he sounded doubtful.

They said their good-byes, and Randi hung up the phone. She returned to the table and looked at Max thoughtfully. Max looked up from her book, and their eyes met.

"That was Gary," Randi said. "He's picking us up at eight."

"Good," Max said. "I am anxious to see this Ralph. I wonder if he is interested in romance."

Randi looked pained. "Now, don't make too big a thing of this, Max. I mean, you might not even like him. You shouldn't expect too much. It's just a date.

Remember Bubba? You had dates with him, but you didn't have a big romance."

"Yes, I remember," Max replied. "How will I know if I'm in love with this Ralph? What sort of evidence should I look for?"

"Max!" Randi practically yelled. "Love isn't a science!"

The sound of the doorbell prevented her from pursuing the matter. "I'll get it," she muttered, shooting a worried look at Max.

She almost didn't recognize the stocky, middle-aged man standing on the doorstep. Without his police uniform, Officer Bronski looked pretty ordinary.

But she recovered her wits quickly enough to greet him warmly.

"Hi, Officer Bronski," she said. "Gramma didn't tell me you were coming over."

He beamed at her. "We always spend Saturdays together," he said happily. He indicated the basket he was carrying, out of which a bunch of daffodils were peeking. "It's such a beautiful day, I thought an impromptu picnic was in order."

Randi eyed the basket doubtfully. "C'mon in," she said. "I'll call her."

But she didn't need to. Just then, her grandmother came bustling down the stairs.

"Carl! What are you doing here?"

He pulled the daffodils out of the basket and held them out to her. "It's Saturday, isn't it? I thought we'd have a picnic."

Gramma didn't even notice the flowers, and she

33

looked pained. "Carl, you should have called first. I have a meeting this afternoon."

Disappointment was clearly reflected on his face. "But we always spend our Saturdays together!"

"Yes, yes, I know," Gramma said, "but this is an important meeting. And I have to run—I'm late already. Why don't you stop by later?" And without waiting for a reply, she waved her hand gaily at all of them and ran out of the house.

Officer Bronski stood there uncomfortably, still clutching the flowers. He looked sad, and Randi felt a wave of sympathy for him.

"Would you like a cup of coffee or something?" she offered.

He shook his head. "No, thanks," he said heavily. He looked at Randi sadly. "Sometimes I think your grandmother takes me for granted."

Randi didn't know how to respond to that. Max wandered into the living room just then, and Officer Bronski seemed to perk up.

"Ah, Max," he said brightly. "How are you?"

"I am fine," Max said briefly, and walked over to the bookcase. She replaced the book she was holding, picked out another, and began to walk out of the room.

"Just a minute, Max," Officer Bronski said, pleasantly but firmly. "I have something to ask you."

Max turned and looked at him. Her expression was apprehensive, but her voice was polite. "Yes?"

"Have you had any progress in recovering from your amnesia? Do you remember anything from your past life?"

Max and Randi exchanged quick looks. Max's eyes were wide, but her voice was calm. "No. I remember nothing."

Officer Bronski eyed her keenly. "I've examined records and reports of runaways and missing children. None of the descriptions resemble you."

Max nodded. "Thank you," she said politely, and turned to leave the room.

"Just a minute," Officer Bronski said again. Max stopped but she didn't turn around. "I find this all very bewildering," he continued. Although her back was to him, his eyes seemed to penetrate her, and slowly she turned and faced him.

"Surely," he said, "someone must be missing you."

Max looked at him steadily. "Perhaps I am an orphan," she said.

Officer Bronski returned her stare without flinching. "But then, you would have been in some sort of institution. And that institution would have filed a missing persons report."

Max glanced at Randi, but Randi was trying as hard as possible to look impassive. This was what she had been fearing—that someone would take it upon himself to investigate Max.

"I am afraid I cannot help you," Max said stonily. "I do not know who I am, or where I am from."

"Well, sooner or later we'll find out who you are," Officer Bronski replied. His tone was pleasant, but Randi couldn't help but shiver. If she, and Gramma, and Max could keep the secret, there was no way he could ever learn the truth about Max. But he seemed so insistent. . . .

"Max will be fine with us," she found herself saying. "There's no need for you to concern yourself."

Officer Bronski smiled at her, but that keen look was still in his eyes.

"But her family may be very worried about her," he said.

"I doubt that," Max said distinctly. Then she whirled around and left the room.

Officer Bronski's eyes followed her for a second, and then he turned to Randi.

"Has Max said anything which might give you any indication as to her past?"

Inside, Randi was shaking, but she managed to face Officer Bronski squarely.

"No."

He sighed. Something about his expression made her think he didn't believe her. But he didn't press the question.

"Well, I'd better be going," he said. "I'll be seeing you soon. I hope." He smiled. "How many committees is your grandmother on?"

"Zillions," Randi replied, forcing a smile. "But I'm sure she'll be able to fit you in."

Briefly he returned the smile and headed for the door. Randi breathed a sigh of relief when he left, and then joined Max in the kitchen.

"He's a nice man," she said to Max, "but he's too curious. I mean, he makes me nervous."

Max's voice was unconcerned. "There is no possible way that he can discover my origins. On my planet there is no such entity as parents. There is no one who will report my disappearance. Certainly such information could never reach Earth. Eventually he will tire of this mystery. And others will not concern themselves with my past."

Except my parents, Randi thought. But she firmly brushed that fear aside. She had at least two weeks before her parents returned from their dig. By then she'd figure out some sort of plan.

Max wandered over to the gilt-edged mirror in the hallway and began examining herself critically. She tugged at her short hair, and an expression of displeasure crossed her face.

"What's the matter?" Randi asked.

Max frowned. "In all the novels I have read, the female has long, luxurious, silken hair that drifts to her shoulders in enticing waves."

Randi stifled a giggle. Max was obviously reciting from memory a description from one of the romances she had been reading.

"I wouldn't worry about that, Max," Randi assured her. "Short hair is very fashionable right now. Besides, your hair will grow eventually."

Max shook her head. "No, I am afraid it will not. It is one of the physical attributes of my species. Our hair only grows to the length you see."

"Oh." Randi smiled apologetically. She kept forgetting that Max wasn't entirely human.

"Tell me," Max said, still examining her image, "is long, luxurious, silken hair a condition necessary for love?"

"Of course not!" Randi exclaimed.

"Good," Max said seriously. "I feared my physical makeup might prohibit me from experiencing a passionate romance."

"Max," Randi asked suddenly, "why is it so terribly important for you to fall in love?"

Max replied promptly. "Because it's something that's very human. And I have no knowledge of it at all. It is something which is totally unfamiliar to me."

Randi looked at her quizzically. "Is there really no such thing as love where you come from?"

"That is correct," Max replied. "As I have told you, in my culture, the male and female are paired in accordance with compatible genetic structures, exclusively for the purpose of reproduction. Obviously, there can be no meaningful relationship, when emotions are considered something to be avoided. Once the man and woman have fulfilled their function, they need not even see each other again!"

"Wow," Randi breathed in wonderment. She couldn't even imagine a world without love.

"So I am eager to discover what love is like," Max continued. "Perhaps I will find out tonight!"

"Now, wait a minute," Randi said hastily, but Max wasn't listening. She started humming something that sounded familiar, and as she left the room, her walk had an odd little skip to it.

Randi stared after her as she drifted upstairs. Max's

voice drifted back down to the hallway. She was singing, and the words were clearly audible.

*"I'm in love, oh, yes, and I feel wonderful . . ."*

Randi listened uneasily. So Max wanted to find out what love was all about. Well, there wasn't anything wrong with that. Everyone wanted to be in love.

But she hoped Max wasn't pinning her hopes on this blind date. From the way Gary had described his cousin—she sincerely doubted that tonight would provide Max with much of an explanation.

# Chapter Four

"My, don't you both look nice!"

Gramma stood in the doorway of Randi's bedroom and beamed at the two girls. "What are you two up to this evening?"

"Gary's cousin Ralph is in town," Randi said as she gave her hair one last brush. "So the four of us are going out. I think we're going to a video arcade."

Max managed to tear her eyes away from her reflection in the mirror to look at Randi.

"What is a video arcade?"

"Oh, it's just a big room where there are all these electronic games. You turn knobs and try to shoot down rockets and stuff," Randi explained vaguely.

When Max looked mildly alarmed, she hastily added, "On a screen, Max. They're not real rockets."

"You know, I tried one of those games myself once," Gramma said, "and to be perfectly honest, I can't figure out why some people enjoy them so much."

"Neither can I," Randi said with a sigh. "But Gary's cousin does, and that's what he wants to do."

"I know nothing of these video games," Max said, "but perhaps that is fortunate. I will appear helpless, and he will attempt to teach me how to play. That should satisfy his male ego."

She turned back to her own reflection and began batting her eyelashes furiously. "Oh, Ralph," she said in a high, giggly voice, "I just can't work these knobs. My little hands can't move them. And you're so much bigger and stronger than I am. Will you help me, pretty please?"

Randi and Gramma both stared at her.

"Max!" Gramma exclaimed. "What are you saying?"

"Where did you pick *that* up?" Randi asked, aghast.

Max turned to her innocently. "I'm imitating a movie I saw on television last night."

Randi rolled her eyes.

"Well, it must have been a very old movie," Gramma retorted. "Women just don't act like that anymore."

Max frowned. "How do women act now?"

"Well, not like *that*." Randi sighed. "Look, Max, just be yourself," and then she bit her lower lip. "I mean . . . just try to be as human as possible." Max still looked puzzled, but Randi didn't know what else to add. She turned to her grandmother.

"Gramma, are you going out with Officer Bronski tonight?"

Her grandmother's face clouded over. "I'm not

sure," she said in a puzzled tone. "We usually do go out on Saturday nights, but he hasn't called. And he did seem somewhat disgruntled when I left this afternoon."

"I think he was disappointed about the picnic," Randi said. "Maybe he thinks you spend too much time on committees and not enough with him."

"Nonsense," Gramma said briskly. "It's true that I'm a very busy woman, but I have seen Carl every Saturday for the past month. And some Sundays, too!"

"Maybe he doesn't think that's enough," Randi said mildly.

"Humph," Gramma snorted. "Well, I'm very fond of Carl Bronski, but I am not about to change my entire lifestyle for *any* man!" And with that she left the room.

Randi had a sinking feeling that by offering advice she had just made the whole situation worse. When would she learn to stop poking her nose into other people's relationships?

Max was looking out the window. "I believe they have arrived," she announced. Her normally placid voice actually held a faint note of excitement. Randi hurried over to the window and peered out.

Gary had just gotten out of the driver's side of the car, and the passenger door was opening. By the dim light of the street lamp, she couldn't get a good look at the infamous cousin, but he appeared to be of average height and build, with dark hair.

"Now, Max," Randi said as she watched the two

figures approach the house, "remember to talk normally tonight. Not that *I* mind the way you talk around here, but it makes other people ask questions about where you're from."

"Right," Max replied. "I got it. I'll talk like you guys."

Randi patted her shoulder gratefully. "Great," she said. "And don't expect too much, okay? I mean, he might not be the boy of your dreams."

Max eyed her solemnly. "People of my species do not dream."

"That's right, I forgot," Randi replied. "But you know what I mean."

The doorbell rang, and Randi started for the door. Max took one last glance into the mirror and tugged uselessly on her hair. "Is there anything else I should remember?"

Randi smiled. "No, just be yourself. But—emphasize the human part."

The girls ran downstairs. Max waited in the living room while Randi answered the door.

"Hi," Gary said. "Hope I'm not late." He was smiling, but the smile looked strained, as if he was struggling to keep it on his face.

"Right on time," Randi said, eyeing him curiously. "C'mon in."

"Randi, this is my cousin Ralph," he said, indicating the boy who followed him inside.

"Hi, Ralph." She gave him a quick once-over. Not bad-looking, she decided. Neat, carefully combed hair, dark eyes, regular features. He was wearing

43

beige trousers and one of those jerseys with a little animal sewed on the front. Definitely preppy, she thought.

"So you're Gary's girl," he said with a cocky grin.

Randi wanted to retort that she wasn't anyone's *girl,* but she resisted the impulse. She didn't want to get the evening off to a bad start.

She led the boys into the living room, where Max stood stiffly in front of the fireplace.

"Ralph," Randi said formally, nervously, "this is my friend Max. Max, this is Gary's cousin Ralph." Thank goodness there was no need for last names. Max didn't have one.

She glanced quickly back and forth between them to judge their reactions. Max looked serious, as if she was critically evaluating his looks. Ralph looked bemused, as if he'd never seen anyone who looked quite like Max. Which he probably hadn't.

"Pleased to meet you," he said briefly. Then he looked around the room. "Nice house."

Max looked startled. "You can see it?"

Ralph stared at her. "Huh?"

Max turned to Randi. "I thought you said he was blind."

Randi groaned silently, and then uttered a quick artificial laugh. "Ha-ha, very funny, Max." She turned to Ralph, who was still staring at Max in disbelief. "Max has a zany sense of humor. Blind date, and all that. You'll get used to it."

Not if I can help it, his expression seemed to say.

44

Gary was tapping his foot impatiently. "Why don't we get going?"

"Right," Randi replied quickly. "Uh, Max, let's go upstairs and get our purses."

Max followed her out of the room and upstairs. Once they were out of earshot, Randi hissed, "I thought you said you read a book about a blind date."

Max looked at her blankly. "I did. He couldn't see, and she had to lead him around."

Quickly Randi explained the usual definition of *blind date*.

"I see," Max said. "It's a figure of speech. Well, it is of no importance. He is an attractive person, but I do not feel any stirrings of passion in my heart."

Randi made a mental note to get Max some higher quality romance books. She grabbed their purses, and the girls went back downstairs.

"All ready," she said brightly, and tried to smile reassuringly at Gary, who was still looking grim.

The four of them walked silently out to Gary's car. Ralph and Max got in the back, and Randi joined Gary up front. She turned her head to Ralph.

"Gary says your family's moving to Riverside," she said conversationally. "Will you be starting at Riverside High in the fall?"

Ralph looked a little bored. "I doubt it. I've always gone to private schools. Public schools are so, you know . . ." He didn't finish the sentence, but the expression on his face made that unnecessary.

Randi glanced at Gary. He was staring straight

45

ahead, at the road, and his face was expressionless. She turned back to Ralph. "Riverside High's okay," she said lightly. "Uh, are you into sports or anything?"

"Yeah, I play a lot of tennis at the club back home," he said. "By the way, is there a decent country club around here?"

"Gee, I don't know," Randi replied honestly. "But there are tennis courts at the community center."

Ralph looked as if the very idea were distasteful. "You mean, a place that's open to *anyone?* Forget it."

Randi couldn't believe a snob like this could be related to Gary. She glanced at Max. Now she was staring at Ralph as if *he* were from outer space.

"Then you are superior to other people?" There was no hostility in her voice; in fact, she sounded innocently curious.

Ralph looked at her blankly. He seemed totally incapable of providing a response to that, and he changed the subject abruptly.

"What's Max short for?"

Now Max looked blank, and Randi held her breath.

"Max is my name," she said simply.

Ralph looked at her as if she were unbelievably stupid.

"But it's not your *real* name," he said.

"No," Max said calmly. "It's not my real name. I don't know my real name. I have amnesia."

Ralph visibly flinched and moved closer to the door.

"I don't know who I am or where I'm from," she

continued. "Randi found me last month and took me home with her."

Ralph looked like he'd lost all powers of speech. Finally he said, "That's really weird."

He sounds like Desiree Dupont, Randi thought. In fact, those two would probably make a perfect couple. She was beginning to feel like this evening was going to be a total disaster.

Gary, who'd been silent throughout the entire ride, finally spoke. "We're here."

He parked the car in front of the video arcade. Ralph visibly brightened. He turned to Max. "You like video games?"

"I don't know," Max replied. "I've never played them. Or maybe I have—but I don't remember."

A condescending half-smile crossed Ralph's face. "I just won a major tournament back home."

"Then I'm sure you'll beat all of us," Randi said with false cheerfulness as they got out of the car. That prospect seemed to improve Ralph's spirits enormously.

The arcade wasn't very crowded. Max wandered ahead of them, gazing at the various games with avid curiosity. As soon as she was out of earshot, Ralph turned to Gary and scowled.

"I thought you said she was good-looking," he muttered in a voice dripping with annoyance.

Gary seemed surprised. "*I* think she's good-looking. Sort of different."

Ralph rolled his eyes. "*Different*'s the word, all

47

right. She looks like some sort of punk rocker. Definitely not my type."

Randi could just imagine what his type was like. And she couldn't believe how rude he was, talking about Max like that right in front of her friends.

"Max is *not* a punk rocker," she said coldly. "And her taste in fashion just shows how independent she is. She's—she's more open-minded than average girls."

Ralph seemed interested in this comment. "Oh yeah? Just how open-minded *is* she?" He leered at Gary. "Hey, maybe this evening won't be so deadly after all."

Randi's mouth fell open. Was he thinking what she thought he was thinking? "Now, hold on," she sputtered, but Max returned before she could set him straight.

"I've never seen anything like this," she said, her eyes wide.

Ralph seemed to be looking at her in a different way, and Randi didn't like it. Then he quickly surveyed the room with a professional eye.

"Max and I will start with Space Destroyers," he announced authoritatively. Then he threw his arm possessively over her shoulders. "C'mon, babe, let's go."

Max turned her head slightly and looked at the hand resting on her shoulder. Then she looked at Ralph in an odd, sort of amused way. But she didn't remove his hand, and she allowed him to walk her over to a game.

Randi watched them with a sense of alarm and turned to Gary.

"He'd better not try anything with her," she hissed.

Gary looked at her with tired resignation on his face. "He's such a creep, there's no telling what he'll try. I'm sorry about this, Randi,"

Randi managed a smile. "It's not your fault," she assured him. "But we'd better keep an eye on them. Let's play whatever that game is next to their's."

The game was Cosmic Collision. Gary pulled a quarter out of his pocket and offered it to Randi.

"You wanna go first?" he asked halfheartedly.

"No, you play," Randi said. She wanted to listen to Ralph and Max.

She pretended to watch Gary, while trying to hear what Ralph was saying to Max. They were only a few feet away, but the noise from the machines made it difficult for her to hear. She edged a few steps away from Gary and strained to hear.

"It's all a matter of dexterity," Ralph was saying. "You have to be able to focus your eyes on the screen and move the knob at the same time."

"I'm not sure I understand," Max replied.

Ralph snickered unpleasantly. "Yeah, girls have a hard time with these complicated maneuvers. This is how it works. See, you're the rocket, and you have to shoot down these alien spaceships. But you also have to watch for these falling meteors. If one of them hits you, you're destroyed. Get it?"

"Gosh, I don't know," Max said in a babyish voice. "It's so complicated. Will you help me?"

She sounded completely helpless. Randi battled an urge to whirl around and kick her. How could she flirt with such a jerk?

"Sure, I'll help you," Ralph replied. "I'll teach you everything I know." His voice dropped, so Randi could just barely hear the next words. "And not just about video games either."

Randi felt sick. She turned slightly so she could actually watch them.

Ralph was positioning Max in front of the game. He stood behind her and placed his hands over hers.

"Now," he said, "I'll be actually operating the controls. But this way, you'll get a feel for the game."

And *you'll* get a feel of Max, Randi thought angrily. She glanced at Max's face to see how she was responding. Her expression was unreadable.

"What's the highest score?" Max asked.

"Fifty thousand," Ralph said, "but it's just about impossible to get a perfect score on this one. Even *I've* never scored higher than forty-five." Again his voice dropped to a seductive low. "Of course, I'm a pretty good scorer in *other* areas, too."

Randi gritted her teeth. Couldn't Max tell that he was coming on to her? How could she just stand there and take it?

Ralph removed one hand from Max's just long enough to stick a quarter into the machine. Randi noticed how his hands were tightening on hers as he manipulated the knobs.

"There's the first spaceship," he said. "Got it! Now here come more—watch out! It's a meteor!"

"Here," Gary said. "It's your turn."

Randi reluctantly removed her eyes from Ralph and Max and stared dismally at Cosmic Collision. It was impossible to keep her mind on the game, especially since she kept turning away from it to see what was going on with Ralph and Max. Needless to say, her score was abysmal, but she didn't care.

When she finished, she saw that Gary had wandered over to watch them. Randi joined them.

"Max is going to play her first game by herself," Ralph said in a patronizing voice. "She *thinks* she's ready."

He handed her a quarter.

"Thank you," Max said sweetly. She put the quarter into the slot, and the spaceships started coming.

*Zap! Zap!* Randi couldn't believe her eyes. Max was hitting those spaceships faster than humanly possible. It was like watching a movie set in fast motion. No meteor came even close to hitting her rocket. And when she finished, the machine erupted in sounds of bells ringing and whistles blowing.

The other three stared at the score on the screen in awe.

"Fifty thousand," Gary murmured unbelievingly. "Isn't that—perfect?"

Max turned to Ralph with an innocent, wide-eyed expression.

"Did I do all right?"

Ralph was staring at the screen in disbelief. A scowl appeared momentarily on his face, but he recovered quickly.

"It looks like I'm a pretty good teacher," he said smugly. "Of course, this is one of the easier games."

"Would you like to play again?" Max asked.

Ralph yawned and looked bored. "Nah. I guess I'm not much in the mood for games after all. At least, not *these* games."

He shot a *significant* look at Max. She seemed oblivious to it.

"How about a movie?" Randi suggested.

Gary glanced at his watch. "Too late for that."

Ralph snapped his fingers, as if a brilliant idea had just occurred to him. "Hey, Randi, is anyone home at your place?"

Randi eyed him suspiciously. "Probably not," she said, figuring her grandmother had probably gone out with Officer Bronski. "Why?"

Ralph grinned. "Let's just go back there and watch television . . . or something." That "or something" made Randi raise her eyebrows and give him her own version of a significant look. But then Gary said, "Yeah, that sounds good to me. I'm kind of beat tonight. We could pick up a pizza on the way and bring it with us."

Randi agreed with this plan uneasily. She had a pretty good idea what was going on in Ralph's mind. But at least she and Gary would be there, too.

In the car Ralph sat a lot closer to Max this time and frequently whispered in her ear. Randi could see them in the mirror, but she couldn't hear what Ralph was saying.

After picking up the pizza they went to Randi's. As

she had expected, her grandmother was out. The four of them settled in the den and opened the pizza. Randi turned on the television, set it to the music video station, and they ate silently while they watched.

"Hey, Max," Ralph said casually after polishing off his third slice, "how about showing me the rest of the house?"

Max jumped up. "I'd be glad too," she said in that silly sweet voice. Randi glared at them both and turned to Gary frantically. But he had fallen asleep on the floor.

"There's nothing much to see," she declared, but the two of them were already half out of the room.

"Gary, wake up!"

He opened his eyes. "Wow," he said sleepily, "I'm even more tired than I thought. What's the matter?"

"Ralph asked Max to show him around the house!"

Gary looked at her quizzically. "So?"

"So I don't think we should leave her alone with him! I don't trust him with her!"

Gary grinned. "Yeah, I think I know what you mean. But Max can take care of herself."

"But she's so naive! You don't understand about Max, Gary. She's not like other girls!"

"You mean, because of her amnesia?"

"No!" Randi exclaimed. "It's more than that!" She had a sudden, serious desire to blurt out the truth about Max so Gary would understand why she was so concerned. "Gary, there's something I have to tell you about Max—"

But she didn't get any further. A loud cry of pain

53

brought them both to their feet and racing out the room.

"Max!" Randi called frantically as they ran up the stairs. "Are you okay?"

They both froze at Randi's bedroom doorway. The scene was unbelievable. Max was standing there, perfectly calm, but her fists were clenched. And Ralph was lying on the floor, his hand on his chin, and a combination of shock and pain on his face.

Gary was wide awake now. "What—what happened?"

Max's tone was bland, but Randi could have sworn she saw something like a twinkle in her eyes.

"We had a disagreement," she said.

Ralph pulled himself to his feet. The look he gave Max was one of pure disbelief.

"What are you, some kind of lady boxer or something?" he snarled. "C'mon, Gary, let's get out of here." He stormed out of the room.

Gary looked at Max apologetically. "Sorry about this, Max." Then he turned to Randi. "I guess I'd better get him home. I'll call you tomorrow."

Randi nodded, feeling like she was in a daze. By the time she heard the door close downstairs, she managed to find her voice.

"Max, what happened?" she asked weakly.

Max smiled. "He wanted to teach me all about love. But I do not wish to learn from him."

Randi nodded. She could certainly understand *that*. "But how did he end up on the floor?"

Max's smile broadened.

54

"I know that you are aware of the vast intellectual superiority of my species. However, I did not tell you that we are also possessed of physical capabilities superior to those of humans."

She paused thoughtfully before she continued:

"With your human custom of dating, I believe these capabilities may be very useful."

# Chapter Five

"He was a total nerd, Gramma, a snotty little creep," Randi said the next morning as they ate breakfast. "It's hard to believe he's actually related to Gary."

Her grandmother seemed to be only half-listening. Listlessly she stirred her tea. "He sounds dreadful," she murmured vaguely.

"He was," Randi assured her, and turned to Max. "Didn't you think he was awful?"

Max nodded. "He was not a pleasant companion. And certainly not a boy I wish to have a meaningful relationship with. Of course, I realized that the moment I saw him."

"Really?" Randi looked at her with interest. "How could you tell? I mean, he wasn't a bad-looking guy."

Max looked smug. "There was no tingle. No spark. No—what did my book call it? Oh, yes—electricity."

Randi grinned. "Oh, yeah, I know what you mean. I remember the first time I talked to Gary. Talk about electricity—it was more like fireworks! Of course," she added hastily, "that was just on my part. It was a while before Gary felt it, too."

Max frowned. "Are you saying that both parties may not feel the electricity simultaneously?"

"Sometimes they do," Randi said. "I guess that would be what they call 'love at first sight.' But sometimes it takes longer."

Max shook her head in puzzlement. "This is all very illogical."

Randi shrugged. "Love isn't logical. Is it, Gramma?"

Again, her grandmother didn't look like she was listening. "What, dear?"

"Max wants to know why people don't always fall in love with each other at the same time. And I told her that love isn't always logical."

Gramma's small smile was tinged with sadness. "She's right, Max. Love isn't logical."

Max's expression didn't change, and she shook her head. "There must be logic," she muttered.

Randi was looking at her grandmother curiously. Something about her last words, the tone in her voice, had her concerned.

"Gramma," she began hesitantly, "is everything okay between you and Officer Bronski?"

The older woman brushed Randi's question aside. "Certainly," she said brusquely, but something in her expression left Randi unconvinced. Mind your own business, she warned herself, but she couldn't help worrying about her normally cheerful grandmother.

She kept an eye on both Gramma and Max over the

57

next few days. During the day both she and Max had their regular Monday-through-Thursday baby-sitting jobs, Randi with the Gordon twins, Max with little Barry Weintraub, Bubba's brother. And Gramma was busy with her usual routine of meetings and volunteer work. Everything seemed normal.

But in the evenings, when everyone was home, Randi was aware of a certain mood in the air. Gramma seemed unusually distracted, lost in her own thoughts. Every time the phone rang, she would perk up—but then, when it wasn't Officer Bronski, she would sink into her own quiet world.

And Max, who wasn't ever all that talkative anyway, seemed even more noncommunicative. She was watching a lot of television, particularly when an old romantic movie was on. And she was still reading her romances, but she rarely asked Randi any more questions about love. Instead, she'd read a few pages, then stare thoughtfully into space, as if she were trying to make some sense out of it all.

Randi was beginning to feel like she was the only person in the house who wasn't depressed. True, she hadn't seen much of Gary lately—he'd started working evenings at a gas station. But he called her every night when he got home, and she knew she'd be seeing him on the weekend.

When she came home from the Gordons' late Thursday afternoon, Max and Gramma were watching the news on television.

"Randi, would you and Max mind getting your own

dinner tonight?" Gramma asked. "I'm going out."

"With Officer Bronski?" Randi asked hopefully.

"No," Gramma replied shortly. "I'm meeting some friends." Randi was dying to ask her what was going on with her and Officer Bronski, but she remembered her vow to mind her own business. She joined Max on the sofa and turned her attention to the news.

"A near-disaster was averted today in Chicago when over a hundred teenage girls stormed the stage during a rock concert," the newscaster intoned solemnly. "During a performance of a local band, the musicians narrowly avoided being trampled by young girls through the quick action of several police officers. Our Chicago affiliate caught the scene on camera."

On the screen there appeared the image of countless girls, screaming and waving their hands in the air. Then the camera focused on the frightened face of the handsome singer as the girls began climbing up on the stage.

Max was staring at the screen with her mouth slightly open. When the report was over, she turned to Randi.

"Why did those girls wish to attack the musicians?" she asked. "Was the music so terrible?"

Randi laughed. "No, they're fans. They just wanted to get close to them, I guess. It happens all the time at rock concerts, only it's usually just a few girls."

"I do not understand."

Randi tried to explain. "Lots of girls are madly in love with rock stars. Sometimes they go berserk." She paused, and giggled. "Come to think of it, I don't know what *I'd* do if I ever saw someone like Bruce Springsteen in person."

Now Max looked really interested. "What is so appealing about rock stars?"

"Oh, they're usually pretty great-looking," Randi said. "Or maybe it's just the music." She turned to her grandmother. "What do you think, Gramma?"

Her grandmother smiled. "I don't know anything about rock stars, Randi. But I must admit, there was a time long ago when I squealed a bit over a singer. Frank Sinatra, I think."

Randi tried to picture her grandmother as a groupie, but it was impossible.

"Well, I have to go," Gramma said. "Have you girls any plans for the evening?"

Gary *had* said something vaguely about dropping by that evening after he got off work. But then Randi looked at Max. She was staring vacantly into space, and Randi felt a sudden wave of sympathy for her. Poor Max hadn't had much fun lately.

"Max," she said suddenly, "let's do something to-night. We don't have to baby-sit tomorrow. Let's go out and have some fun."

Max didn't look too enthusiastic, but she nodded. "What would you like to do?"

Randi thought for a minute. "I'm not sure," she said. "I'll go call Ellen and see if she has any bright ideas."

"Well, whatever you do, be careful and have a good time," Gramma said. "I'll see you girls later."

Randi waved good-bye to her as she dialed Ellen's number.

"Ellen? Hi, it's Randi. Are you doing anything tonight?"

"Not particularly. What did you have in mind?"

"I don't know," Randi said. "Max and I were just talking about doing something. You got any ideas?"

"How about checking out that Teen Scene place at the mall?"

"I don't know," Randi said doubtfully. "Is that a place you can go without a date?"

"Sure," Ellen replied. "It's supposed to be very casual."

"I guess we can get up for that," Randi said, glancing across the room at Max, who was still staring into space. "But how are we going to get there and back?"

"I'll bet Karen Shulman would want to go," Ellen said. "And she's got her driver's license. Maybe she can get her parents' car. I'll call her right now and get back to you."

Randi hung up the phone and turned to Max. "Ellen wants to go to the Teen Scene at the mall. It's a club, with live bands and dancing. Does that sound good to you?"

Max seemed to come out of her daze, and she actually looked interested.

"Live bands," she repeated. "Like on the news report?"

"Yeah," Randi replied, "but don't worry—I sincerely doubt that anyone will storm the stage!"

"Yes," Max said thoughtfully, "that sounds like something I would like to do."

Randi raised her eyebrows, and Max looked at her reprovingly. "Not storm the stage," she said. "I mean, I *would* like to go to this Teen Scene."

The phone rang, and Randi grabbed it.

"Hi, it's me." Ellen's voice sounded enthusiastic. "Karen can get the car! We'll pick you guys up at eight, okay?"

"Great!" Randi replied happily. "Hey, this will be fun! A regular girls' night out!" She dialed Gary's number at the garage.

"Hi, it's me."

"Oh, hi Randi. Listen, I'm really not supposed to get personal calls here."

"I'm sorry," Randi said. "I just wanted to tell you, I'm going out with some of the girls tonight."

"Oh," Gary said in a subdued voice. "Gee, I thought maybe I'd drop by later—"

Randi lowered her voice. "I know, but Max has been so down lately. I think she needs a night out. You don't really mind, do you? I mean, it's not as if we had real plans."

"Yeah, I know," Gary said. "Well, we're still going to the carnival tomorrow night, aren't we?"

"Absolutely," Randi promised.

Later, as she and Max were up in her bedroom preparing for the evening, Randi was pleased to note that Max actually seemed excited about the prospect of the Teen Scene.

"What happens at this Teen Scene place?" she asked.

"Oh, you listen to the music, and dance, I guess," Randi said as she poked through her closet. "I've never been there."

"But I do not know how to dance," Max said worriedly, as she put on her hot pink jumpsuit.

"Don't worry," Randi said, pulling a bright Hawaiian print shirt out of her closet. "Dancing's easy. You just sort of sway to the beat. We'll show you."

She had just enough time to slip into the shirt and her jeans before they heard Karen's car honking outside.

The petite, red-haired driver greeted them gaily.

"Hi! Ready to party? I hear this place really swings!"

"Absolutely!" Randi exclaimed. "You know, I haven't danced in ages. I don't think Gary's into it."

"Speaking of Gary," Ellen said, turning around in the front seat to look at Randi, "does he know you're doing this tonight?"

"Sure," Randi said. "But he doesn't mind. I mean, we have an understanding." She smiled complacently. "I don't have to worry about him, and he doesn't worry about me."

"Wish I could find a guy like that," Karen murmured.

"Are you also looking for the experience of love?" Max asked her with avid curiosity.

Karen laughed. "Well, I don't know if that's exactly

what I'm looking for," she said. "I'd just like to find a nice guy to go out with. I'm not up for any heavy, serious commitment."

"Oh." Max thought about this. "I suppose companionship is important. But I want to fall in love."

"Don't we all," Ellen chortled.

Randi listened to this conversation with some mild uneasiness. Karen didn't know the truth about Max, where she was from and all that. Randi hoped Max wouldn't say anything *too* peculiar tonight. Karen was a pretty good friend—in fact, she was on the cheerleading squad with Randi. But she was famous for having a big mouth.

Randi poked Max. When she got her attention, she silently mouthed the words "talk normal." Max nodded to indicate that she understood.

Karen parked the car in the mall parking lot, and the girls headed over to the Teen Scene.

"Hey, look," Ellen said excitedly, pointing at the sign over the door. "Spit's playing."

"Wow!" Karen exclaimed. "I heard them at a dance last year. They're fantastic!"

"Yeah, I know," Randi said, "but remember, where there's Spit, there's Desiree. She's been going out with Chad Bellamy."

"Lucky Desiree," Karen said with a sigh. "He's *so* cute."

"Desiree," Max murmured, and if possible, her face became even paler than usual. Randi remembered how nasty Desiree had been to Max when Max first arrived. "Don't worry about *her*," she said comfortingly. "The place will be so crowded we probably won't even see her. And even if we do, what can she do to you?"

"What are we waiting for?" Karen asked. "Let's go in!"

She opened the door to the club, and the others followed her in. It took them all a moment to get accustomed to the dim lighting.

"Wow," Ellen breathed, "this is *neat!*"

Randi echoed her sentiments. The place was really something—red walls, a black ceiling with tiny lights that looked like stars, a chrome soda bar running around the perimeter. A few steps down was the dance floor, crowded with couples gyrating to the blaring of music from unseen loudspeakers. Others were gathered in clumps around the bar. Randi spotted some kids from school and waved to them. Karen drifted over to talk to them.

"Where is the band?" Max asked.

"They probably don't start playing till later," Randi replied. "Let's get a soda."

Max and Ellen followed her to the bar, where they ordered their drinks. Randi felt terribly sophisticated as she leaned against the bar, sipping her soda and watching the dancers.

"This is just like a real disco," she marveled.

"Yeah," Ellen said happily. "And I see some sharp-looking guys over there." She indicated another part of the bar.

"Well, they certainly don't interest me," Randi said primly. She turned to Max. "But maybe you'll find the love of your life."

Max didn't even look in their direction. "I'm waiting for the band," she said. Randi shot her a curious look. Why was Max suddenly so interested in music?

Karen joined them at the bar. "Don't look now, but guess who just walked in?"

Randi didn't have to guess. The subject of Karen's remark was sauntering toward them.

"Hi, Desiree," she said, managing a reasonably pleasant smile.

Desiree didn't bother with small talk. "What are you girls doing here?" She made it sound like they weren't exactly welcome.

"Just thought we'd check this place out," Ellen said lightly. "I like your outfit."

Desiree accepted the compliment as her just due. Randi had to admit Desiree did look terrific, if a little too glitzy. She had on a black sequined T-shirt and her stirrup pants were dotted with sequins too.

"Where's Chad?" Karen asked.

"He's with the band, setting up," Desiree replied. "They're going to be so hot tonight. They've got three new numbers and—" She stopped speaking abruptly. Randi realized that she had just noticed Max.

Desiree's eyes narrowed ominously, and Randi held her breath. But Max handled it all pretty well.

"Hello," Max said politely, and then turned to the others. "Excuse me, I'm going to the ladies' room."

Desiree watched her walk away, and then focused her stony look on Randi.

"When is she going back to wherever-it-is she's from?"

Randi shrugged. "I guess whenever she finds out where that is. Remember, she's got amnesia."

"I remember," Desiree said grimly. She tossed her head and pushed her blond hair off her shoulder. "Listen, girls, we need to have a meeting of the Stars before school starts. I'll call you about it. And Randi, when we have this meeting . . ."

"Yes?"

"It's members only." With that, she whirled around and headed for the stage beyond the dance floor.

"Whew," Karen said, "she's not too crazy about Max, is she? How come?"

Randi didn't feel like going into the whole story. "Oh, she thinks Max had something to do with breaking up her and Gary. It's sort of funny—she doesn't care that I'm going out with Gary, and she's not even interested in him anymore now that she's got Chad. But she's got this grudge against Max. I think it's just because Max is different, and she's not the type to do what Desiree tells her to."

"Like we do," Ellen said abruptly. Randi and Karen looked at her with startled expressions. There was a moment of silence.

"You're right," Randi said reluctantly, "we do let Desiree push us around. And she's not even a good friend!"

"True," Karen said, "but she's president of the Stars, and captain of the cheerleading squad. And we're all members of the Stars, and we're all cheerleaders. So like her or not, Desiree's got a lot of power."

The three of them sighed in unison.

"Maybe I should go get Max and tell her the coast is clear," Randi said, but that proved to be unnecessary. Max emerged from the ladies' room and joined them.

"Is it time for the band yet?" she asked.

Her question was answered over the loudspeakers.

"And here they are—live and in person—Riverside's hottest band—Spit!"

The lights went up on the stage, an explosion of frantic drumming, a clash of cymbals, and the band burst into their first number.

"They *are* good." Randi had to yell to be heard over the music.

"Which one is Chad Bellamy?" Ellen screamed.

"I think he's the one in the black jacket with the gold braid!" Randi yelled back. She started to ask Max how she liked it so far, but the girl wouldn't look at her. She seemed completely transfixed by the band.

Chad Bellamy stepped up to the mike and started to sing. He didn't have a particularly great voice—actually, he sounded more like he was growling than singing. But he was so great-looking, it didn't really matter. His hair was longer than most guys in Riverside, but on him it looked good—straight blond hair which brushed over his eyes. He was thin and wiry, and when he moved, he looked unbelievably sexy.

"I feel like dancing!" Karen yelled.

"Me too," Randi said.

"Who with?" Ellen asked.

"We can dance with each other," Karen said.

"Look." And she pointed toward the dance floor. Sure enough, there were a lot of girls dancing together.

"Okay," Ellen said. "Let's go!"

"Max? Do you want to dance?" Karen asked.

Max blinked. "Yes." As the four of them moved out on the dance floor, she said to Randi, "I have been observing the dancers, and I believe I have figured out how it is done."

She wasn't kidding. When they found an empty spot on the dance floor, near the band, Max took off. She was incredible—like a professional dancer. She kicked, she twirled, she moved her hips like she'd been dancing for years.

"She obviously remembers how to dance!" Karen yelled at Randi. Randi managed to smile and nod. She'd forgotten how quickly Max could learn anything.

The evening flew by. The band played a lot of the current hit songs, and the audience was enthusiastic. Randi hadn't danced so much in ages. When the band finally took a break, she realized she was exhausted.

"Whew, I'm beat," she gasped. The others agreed, and they retreated to the bar.

"I'm going to need to get the car back pretty soon," Karen said. "Are you kids about ready to take off?"

"Yeah," Randi said. "It's been fun, but I think I've danced enough. Do we have time for one more drink?"

"I could use one, too," Ellen said, still out of breath.

As she drank her soda Randi realized someone was missing.

"Where's Max?"

Karen and Ellen both looked blank. "I thought she was with us," Ellen said.

Randi felt uneasy. The place was even more packed than it had been an hour before, and she was afraid Max might be lost in the crowd. "I'm going to look for her," she said suddenly. "You guys stay here, or we'll never find each other."

She made her way through the crowd, looking around. The dance floor was less crowded now that records were being played again, and Max wasn't down there. Then she glimpsed a flash of hot pink next to the stage and began walking in that direction.

It *was* Max, and she was just standing there, absolutely still, like a statue.

"Max? What are you doing?"

Max didn't reply. Her eyes seemed to be fixed on something, somebody actually, adjusting something on a guitar. When the figure turned around, Randi could see that it was Chad Bellamy. He noticed Max standing there.

"Hi." It was just a tiny one-syllable word, but Chad's pouty lips made it sound like an invitation to— who knew what? And Max had the most peculiar smile on her face.

Randi nervously looked around for any trace of Desiree. If she was witnessing this encounter, a major crisis was imminent.

"Max," she called urgently. Max didn't seem to

hear her. "Max!" Finally she turned. "C'mon, we're going."

Max nodded, and then looked again at Chad. A slow smile spread across his face. "See ya around," he said.

Max just looked at him. Then she spun around and began walking briskly toward Randi.

"I'm ready to go," she said. There was an unusual exuberance in her voice, and Randi eyed her apprehensively.

"Max," she asked tentatively, "why were you looking at him like that?"

Max seemed mildly surprised by the question. "He is a rock star, yes?"

"Well, not a star," Randi demurred. "But I guess he's the closest thing Riverside has to a celebrity. Why?"

Max looked satisfied. "I think I can fall in love with him."

Randi stared at her, aghast. "Max! You don't even know him!"

Max's expression didn't change. "Did those girls on television today know the rock stars?"

Randi was bewildered. "No," she managed to say.

"And you said many girls fall madly in love with rock stars. Chad Bellamy is a rock star. Therefore, I believe I could be in love with him."

Randi couldn't think of anything to say. She just stood there, eyes wide, mouth open. Max smiled patiently and patted Randi on the shoulder.

"It is all very logical."

# Chapter Six

"Are you telling me that Max has a crush on *Chad Bellamy?*" The voice on the other end of the line sounded incredulous.

"Ellen, I can't believe it either," Randi said. "But you saw how she was acting in the car last night on the way home. Completely spaced out."

"Yeah, I noticed," Ellen admitted, "but I thought she was just, you know, being Max. Only more so."

"I tried to talk to her when we got home," Randi said. "I explained to her that when girls get crushes on rock stars, it's usually the music that gets to them, not necessarily the guy. But she's got this wacky idea that Chad's the boy she's been waiting for, and she won't listen to me."

"What are you going to do about this?"

"There's nothing I *can* do," Randi replied. "Once Max has made her mind up about something . . . I'm just afraid she's going to get hurt."

"I know what you mean," Ellen said. "I doubt that Chad's going to call her or anything. He and Desiree seem to have a pretty heavy thing going."

Randi agreed. "And if he did call, I'm still afraid she'd get hurt. He's got a reputation for running around, doesn't he?"

"That's what I've heard," Ellen said. "Well, don't worry about it. Desiree's got her hooks into him, and I sincerely doubt that she's going to let him go any time soon. And Max will get over it. Where is she today, anyway?"

"Oh, she's home," Randi said. "She's downstairs watching music videos. I think she's giving herself a crash course in rock 'n' roll—so she'll have something in common with Chad." She sighed heavily. "Of all the guys in the world for her to fall for. . . ."

When she got off the phone, Randi ran downstairs to check on Max. On the way she passed her grandmother, who was sitting at the kitchen table stirring a cup of tea and staring blankly into space.

Max was completely engrossed by the television. Her expression was so intense that Randi decided not to disturb her.

When she passed the kitchen on her way back upstairs, she noticed that Gramma was still stirring her tea, and still staring at nothing.

"Gramma?" The older woman looked up, startled. "That tea's going to get cold if you don't drink it."

Gramma looked down at her cup as if noting for the first time that it was even there. Randi joined her in the kitchen and pulled up a chair.

"What's wrong, Gramma? Are you feeling okay? You look really out of it."

Her grandmother shook her head wearily and started to say "it's nothing," but this time Randi was too concerned to mind her own business.

"C'mon, Gramma," she said encouragingly. "Whatever's bugging you, you might feel better if you talk about it."

Her grandmother managed a little smile, but it was only a weak imitation of her usual cheerful expression. She seemed to be debating whether or not to confide in Randi.

"Carl hasn't called," she finally admitted. "And I suppose I'm feeling a little depressed about it."

"What happened between you guys anyway?" Randi asked curiously.

Her grandmother sighed deeply. "Carl wanted me to give up some of my activities, my committees and volunteer work, so I could spend more time with him. I told him that I like my life just the way it is, and I don't intend to make any changes in it."

Randi pondered this. "Gramma," she began hesitantly, "you like him a lot, don't you?"

Her grandmother nodded.

Randi decided to pursue this. "Do you . . . *love* him?"

A slow blush crept over her grandmother's plump face. She didn't answer that, but Randi thought she could see the answer in her eyes.

"Have you told him how you feel about him?" Randi asked.

Her grandmother looked a little shocked at that idea. "Good heavens, no. After all, we've only been seeing each other a few weeks. I hardly think it's appropriate at this point in time to reveal my feelings."

Randi almost started laughing, but managed to restrain herself. "You know, Gramma, for a modern, up-to-date lady, you've got some pretty old-fashioned ideas."

Her grandmother raised her eyebrows indignantly. "And what do you mean by that, young lady?"

"It's *okay* to say what you feel," Randi said spiritedly. "Remember when we were talking about silly romantic games? Nowadays, you don't have to play those games anymore. If you care about a guy, you tell him—you don't have to play hard-to-get."

"And what do you expect me to do? Jump in the car, drive to his house, and throw myself at him?"

Now Randi *did* laugh. "Of course not. But you could call him, invite him over, and have a good, long heart-to-heart."

Her grandmother took a sip of tea, and then made a face. "Ice cold," she murmured.

"Well?" Randi persisted. "Are you going to call him?"

Her grandmother was silent for a minute. "I don't know. . . . After all, he hasn't called me. And I do have *some* pride."

Randi suddenly felt like *she* was the older, more experienced one.

"Pride can kill a relationship, Gramma," she said wisely.

The woman gave her a half-amused, half-serious look. "How did you get so smart all of a sudden?" Then she chuckled lightly. "Well, maybe I'll call him. . . . We'll see." Then she looked around. "By the way, where's Max? I haven't seen her around all day."

Randi grimaced. "She's hooked on music videos. She's down in the den watching TV."

Her grandmother glanced at the clock. "But it's almost five o'clock! Are you telling me she's been in the house all day watching TV?"

Randi nodded. She didn't want to explain Max's sudden interest in rock 'n' roll to her grandmother. She had her own problems to think about.

"Are you girls going out tonight?"

"Well, I'm going to the carnival with Gary," Randi said. The carnival came to town for a week every August, and for that one week it was *the* place to be.

"Why don't you take Max with you," her grandmother suggested. "At least that would get her away from the television set."

Randi hesitated before answering. She wasn't sure how Gary would feel about that idea. Just this morning, when she had talked to him on the phone, he kept saying how much he was looking forward to being with her that evening. How would he feel about Max being with them?

On the other hand, she did need to get Max's mind off Chad. And if a carnival couldn't do that . . .

Another thought occurred to her, and she caught her grandmother's eye.

"If I get Max to come along with me and Gary

tonight," she said, her eyes twinkling, "then you can invite Officer Bronski over and have the house to yourselves!"

Her grandmother looked like she was about to object to that—but then she smiled broadly. "We'll see about that," was all she said, but Randi had a suspicion that the idea was not entirely disagreeable to her!

She ran down to the den, where Max was still glued to the TV. "Max," she said, and then, louder, "Max!"

The girl finally, reluctantly, removed her eyes from the TV and turned to Randi. "Yes?"

"Would you like to go to the carnival tonight with Gary and me?"

Max was momentarily distracted by a new video.

"That is Prince," she informed Randi. "He is considered to be highly funky."

"I know, I know," Randi replied impatiently. "Max, did you hear what I asked you?"

Max looked at her blankly, and Randi repeated the invitation.

"What is a carnival?" Max asked, with only mild interest.

"Mostly games, and rides, and lots of junk food."

"I see." Max sounded completely unenthused. "I prefer to stay home and study this music. There is a special program tonight which will feature heavy metal."

Randi groaned. "Max, I can tell you all you need to know about heavy metal. It's *loud*. C'mon, the carnival's only here for a week. And it's a lot of fun, really."

Max didn't respond, but Randi had a sudden inspiration. "And I *think*," she said casually, "that a rock band might be performing there."

*That* got Max's attention. "Will Chad Bellamy be there?" she asked eagerly.

Randi rolled her eyes. "I don't know. . . . Look, Max, you've got to stop thinking about Chad Bellamy. For crying out loud, you don't even know him! And besides, he goes with Desiree, and—no offense, Max—but I don't think he's going to leave her for you. Not that Desiree's any better than you," she added hastily, "but they seem to have a serious relationship. And I just can't see you and Chad getting together."

Max didn't bat an eyelash. "Love conquers all," she said solemnly.

"Max!" Randi practically shrieked. "That's in a soap opera! It's not real life! Besides, love is when two people feel the same about each other. What makes you think Chad's interested in you?"

Max smiled confidently. "I could see it in his eyes— just like in the movies. It was love at first sight."

Randi didn't want to be cruel, but she figured she had to bring Max back to earth.

"Max," she said gently, "if he's in love with you— why hasn't he called?"

"That is only logical," Max replied calmly. "He must first dissolve the existing relationship with Desiree before he can declare his true feelings for me."

Randi couldn't think of anything to say. What was the use? Max had made up her mind that she and Chad

78

would be in love, and nothing Randi could say would convince her otherwise.

"Whatever you say," Randi murmured in a resigned voice. "Look, do you want to come to the carnival or not?"

"You say there will be a rock band there?"

Now Randi was getting irritated. "I said *maybe*. . . . Look, Max, don't do me any favors . . ."

Max must have caught the sound of annoyance in Randi's voice, because she suddenly smiled sweetly. "Thank you. I will join you and Gary."

Now all she had to do was inform Gary—and she wasn't looking forward to his reaction when she told him they wouldn't be alone tonight. She went up to the kitchen to call him, but her grandmother was on the phone.

"About eight, then," she was saying. "Good-bye." And she hung up. When she saw Randi, she smiled happily. "That was Carl. I called him, as you suggested."

"Is he coming over?"

Her grandmother nodded.

"Great!" Randi said. "I'm sure you guys will be able to work this out. And Max is coming to the carnival with me and Gary, so you *will* have the house to yourself." Then she grinned impishly. "But don't do anything *I* wouldn't do."

Her grandmother laughed. "I'm just glad you talked me into calling him. He was so surprised! But he sounded pleased. And now I think I'll go have a long, hot bubble bath." She drifted out of the room humming to herself, and Randi patted her own back for having been the impetus for this new mood.

But now she had to call Gary, and her heartbeat quickened as she dialed his number. Surely he'll understand, she told herself, but she wasn't so sure.

"Gary? Hi, it's me." Then, in a rush, before he could even return her greeting, she said, "I asked Max to come with us to the carnival tonight, okay?"

There was a silence on the other end, and for a second Randi thought they had been disconnected. "Gary? Are you there?"

Finally a low voice replied. "Yeah, I'm here. Gosh, Randi, why did you have to go and do that for? I wanted us to be together tonight."

"We'll be together," Randi said.

"Together, *alone,*" Gary replied.

Randi sighed. "I'm sorry, Gary, but I just *had* to get her out of the house tonight. Last night, she met Chad Bellamy at the Teen Scene. And now she's got this crazy crush on him."

"What's that got to do with her coming to the carnival tonight?"

"Well, I want to get her mind off him," Randi replied.

"Look, Randi," Gary said, "you can't control Max's life for her. If she wants to chase after Chad, let her."

"But I have to take care of her," Randi said.

Gary sounded really annoyed. "Haven't we had this conversation before? I know she's got amnesia, but she seems perfectly capable of taking care of herself."

I'm going to have to tell him the truth about her, Randi thought. But not now.

"Gary, please," she said, "I just feel responsible for her, okay? And anyway, there's going to be a huge crowd at the carnival. It's not as if we could really be alone."

"Okay, okay," Gary said, but he didn't sound very agreeable. "I'll pick you guys up at seven-thirty."

And he didn't even wait for Randi's usual "I love you, good-bye" before he hung up.

"Max?" Randi yelled. "Gary's here. Let's go!"

Standing by the living room window, she anxiously watched Gary get out of his car, and tried to read his expression. He didn't look particularly unhappy, and she breathed a sigh of relief when she caught his eye, and he smiled and waved.

She held the door open for him, and he kissed her cheek. "Sorry about the way I sounded this afternoon," he said. "I guess I just don't want to always be sharing you."

"It's just for tonight," Randi promised. "I won't keep bringing her along with us, honest."

"Where is she, anyway?" Gary asked. "I want to get to the fairgrounds so we can get a decent parking space."

"Max!" Randi yelled. "Come *on!*"

Finally she appeared, and Randi had to admit she had made good use of all the time she spent getting ready. She looked terrific, in her hot-pink cropped pants and a wild purple off-the-shoulder T-shirt. Next to Max, Randi felt positively dowdy in her conservative jeans and plaid shirt.

"You look great," Randi said, and Gary obliged with a short whistle.

"I copied a model in a magazine," Max said. "Do you think Chad will like it?"

Randi grimaced. "Max, I don't even know if Chad's going to be there."

"If he doesn't like it, he'd be crazy," Gary said jovially. Randi made a face at him and hissed, "Don't encourage her," but Gary just grinned, and said, "Let's go."

On the way to the carnival Gary turned on the radio, and Max began singing along. Randi was amazed—she seemed to know all the words to every song played.

"Max, you've got a nice voice," Gary remarked.

Max seemed surprised to hear that. "I do?"

"Hasn't anyone ever told you that before?" he asked.

Max shook her head. "I've never sung before. That I'm aware of," she added quickly.

"Oh, that's right," Gary said. "I keep forgetting about your amnesia. That must feel really strange, not having a past, having to learn things from scratch."

Max didn't say anything, and Randi felt uncomfortable. One of these days she was going to have to tell Gary about Max. She was beginning to feel a little guilty about having kept this secret from him for so long.

The parking lot at the fairgounds was already

packed, but Gary managed to find a space. And as they walked toward the entrance to the carnival, Randi felt her spirits lift as she took in the bright lights, the huge roller coaster and Ferris wheel, the crowds, and the noise.

Max was impressed, too. She didn't say much, but her eyes were wide.

"I did not expect anything quite so elaborate," she whispered to Randi as Gary bought their tickets.

"The carnival's a big deal," Randi replied. "It's only here for one week each summer, so everyone gets pretty excited about it."

Max looked puzzled. "But if everyone enjoys it so much, why is it not permanent?"

"I don't know," Randi said vaguely. "Maybe if it were here all the time, people wouldn't like it so much. They'd take it for granted, and it wouldn't be so exciting."

Max looked at her disapprovingly. "That is illogical," she stated flatly. "If something is pleasurable, it should be permanent. Like love."

Randi tried to think of a good comeback for that, but she couldn't. Gary returned with their tickets, and they strolled onto the fairgrounds.

"Look," Randi said, pointing toward a game booth, "there's Bubba."

Her tall, husky next-door neighbor was pitching beanbags at a board, trying to get them into holes. He wasn't having much luck. He greeted them all cheerfully as they approached, but his eyes lingered on Max.

83

He still cares about her a lot, Randi thought as she watched his expression soften. She still wished things had worked out between them. He'd be so much better for her than someone like Chad. She glanced at Max. She seemed oblivious to Bubba's wistful expression. Her eyes were searching the crowds. Probably looking for Chad, Randi thought unhappily.

"You here alone?" Gary asked him.

"Nah," Bubba replied, picking up another beanbag and aiming it carefully. "I've got a date with Christy Feeley. She's on the Ferris wheel." He threw the beanbag. It missed by at least a foot. He shrugged good-naturedly. "Guess pitching was never one of my talents."

"Why aren't you on the Ferris wheel with Christy?" Randi asked curiously.

Bubba seemed reluctant to answer. He grabbed another beanbag and gave it undue consideration before pitching it. He missed again.

"I'm not too crazy about these rides," he said casually. Then he grinned. "To tell you the truth, they make me sick."

The thought of the big, athletic Bubba getting sick on a Ferris wheel would have made Randi giggle except for the fact that he was expressing her own sentiments exactly.

Even Gary was sympathetic. "Yeah, I know what you mean," he said. "That roller coaster over there—I get dizzy just looking at it. I kind of like the Ferris wheel, though."

"How about you, Max?" Bubba asked. "You like those rides?"

Max glanced briefly toward the Ferris wheel and the roller coaster. "They look unimpressive," she said.

"Oh, yeah?" Gary grinned. "C'mon, Randi, I think we should take Max on the Ferris wheel. Maybe she won't think it's so unimpressive when it stops at the top and she realizes how high up we are."

Max smiled slightly. "I've been higher," she murmured. Randi wanted to kick her, but then she got a bright idea.

"Gary, let's just you and me go," she said. "Bubba, why don't you show Max some of these games?"

Bubba looked at Max eagerly. "Want to do that?" Max shrugged impassively.

"C'mon, Gary, let's go," Randi said quickly. "We'll meet you guys back here after the ride, okay?"

As they strolled away Gary looked at her quizzically. "Do you really want to go on that ride, or are you just up to your matchmaking tricks again?"

Randi decided to go for a little white lie. "I'm just looking for an excuse to be alone with you." She eyed him flirtatiously. "Do you mind?"

Gary laughed. "I can handle it," he said.

But as they approached the Ferris wheel, and Randi took in its mammoth structure, she began to feel a little sick.

"Uh, Gary, maybe we could just walk around for a while, or something," she said hesitantly, and looked up at him. He was looking at the line waiting to board the ride.

"Yeah, I know what you mean," he said, and then she realized what he was seeing. Desiree Dupont and Chad Bellamy were standing on line, too.

They both turned abruptly away, but not soon enough.

*"Randi!"*

Randi turned reluctantly and saw Desiree beckoning to her.

"I'd better see what she wants," she murmured to Gary. He rolled his eyes. "I'll wait here," he muttered.

Randi glanced at Chad as she approached them. In a way, she could see why Max was so attracted to him. He was awfully good-looking, with that blond hair and that silver glitter shirt hugging his thin body. But his expression was so sullen—he seemed to be totally bored. Desiree wasn't looking too happy either.

"I just wanted to tell you we're having a Stars meeting tomorrow at my house," she said. "Two o'clock."

Before Randi could even respond to that, Chad turned impatiently to Desiree. "C'mon, baby, let's get out of here," he mumbled. "This place is a drag."

"But I wanna ride the Ferris wheel," Desiree whined. "And besides, I didn't get all dressed up just to sit in your car—" she stopped suddenly, realizing that Randi was still standing there. "I'll see you tomorrow," she said pointedly. Randi nodded and started to walk away. But even as she rejoined Gary, she could still hear Desiree and Chad arguing, their voices rising.

"What's going on?" Gary asked.

Randi shrugged. "We're having a Stars meeting tomorrow." She turned and glanced back at Desiree. Now she and Chad were leaving the line, but their voices had gotten so loud she could still hear them as they walked away. She couldn't quite make out the words, but the tone was definitely angry.

Gary was looking at them, too, and he was shaking his head. "How did I ever go out with her," he was saying, more to himself than to Randi. And then he grinned. "Hey, now we can go on the Ferris wheel!"

Randi's heart sank, but she smiled bravely. "Okay!"

Actually, it wasn't too bad. She held Gary's hand tightly and managed to get through those sickening moments when the wheel stopped and their car swung back and forth. And when their car stopped at the top, she just held her breath and tried not to look down.

"Hey, you can see out over the whole grounds!" Gary was saying happily. "I can even see Max over there."

Randi opened her eyes a crack and looked over in the direction Gary was indicating. But what she saw made her suddenly forget her fears, and her eyes opened wide.

Even though they were just specks on the ground, she could pick out Max because of her golden hair. And the figure that was standing next to her—she had seen that silver glitter shirt just moments before.

"Gary!" she said frantically. "She's with Chad Bellamy!"

"Well, you can't do anything about that from here," Gary said mildly.

It seemed like ages before the Ferris wheel started moving again. Every time the wheel stopped, she looked over toward the place where she had seen Max. But they were too low now, and she couldn't see them anymore.

As soon as they were at the bottom, Randi leaped out of her seat and began to walk rapidly back toward the beanbag toss booth.

"Hey, hold on!" Gary said, sounding a little annoyed. "I thought you wanted us to be alone!"

Randi turned to him impatiently. "Gary, come on! I don't want to leave her alone with Chad."

But when they reached the booth, Max was alone and calmly pitching beanbags at the board. Every one of them landed in a hole, and the girl behind the booth was staring at her with her mouth open.

"I've been running this booth for ten years," she was saying, "and I've never seen anyone do this!" She was looking less than pleased as she handed Max a gigantic stuffed animal. Randi noticed that there were two others on the ground next to Max.

"Max! Are you okay? Where's Bubba?" Randi asked anxiously.

"I sent Bubba away with his date," Max replied calmly. "And yes, I am okay. Have an animal. You too, Gary."

She *did* look okay—better than okay. In fact, there was an unusual glow on her normally pale face.

"Wow, you must be one great pitcher!" Gary exclaimed, looking at Max's prizes in wonderment.

"I have had an exciting experience," Max explained, "and I believe this excitement has improved my dexterity."

Randi eyed her suspiciously. "*What* exciting experience?"

Max smiled placidly. "I have spoken with Chad Bellamy."

Randi's stomach began to churn.

"So?"

Max was looking smug. "What I expected has happened. Chad and Desiree have dissolved their relationship. Or, as he put it so eloquently, they 'broke up.' "

Randi managed to get out a weak "And?"

"And he has asked me for a date. Tomorrow night." Max's eyes were bright with anticipation. "Now," she continued, "I will finally have the experience of love."

Her choice of words *did* cause Gary to look a little surprised. And Randi felt more than a little sick.

# Chapter Seven

"Randi! Wake up!"

The words slowly penetrated Randi's semiconscious brain, and she responded without opening her eyes. "Wha—? Huh?"

"Randi! Please, wake up!"

The urgency in Max's voice forced Randi's eyes open. They widened as she took in the state of their bedroom.

It looked like it had been struck by a tornado. Half the clothes in the closet were strewn over beds, and shoes were all over the floor.

"Max," Randi mumbled in a voice still groggy. "What are you doing?"

Max held a shirt in one hand and a skirt in the other. "Do you think this is an appropriate combination?"

Randi leaned on her elbows and propped herself up. "Appropriate for what?"

Max looked impatient. "For my date with Chad Bellamy, of course!"

Randi turned to look at the clock on the nightstand by her bed. Then she sank back onto her pillow with a loud groan.

"Max, it's seven o'clock in the morning! You're not going out with Chad till tonight!"

"But I have to select the perfect clothing. This is the beginning of my romance, and it is very important that I dress appropriately. Please, Randi, I need your advice on this matter."

Reluctantly Randi pulled herself to a sitting position, rubbed her eyes, and peered closely at the outfit Max was holding. Then she frowned. "Max, that's *my* shirt."

Max looked at her plaintively. "But surely you would not mind if I borrowed it. I will be very careful."

Randi sighed and was about to say okay when Max suddenly shook her head and tossed the shirt back on her bed.

"No, it will not do. It is too dull."

Randi glared at her indignantly. "What do you mean, too dull? I just bought that shirt last week!"

Max was oblivious to Randi's tone. "No, it is inappropriate. I must wear something that complements Chad's appearance, so we will appear to be a perfectly matched set." She scrutinized the piles of clothing carefully. "Do you not have anything that glitters?"

"No, I don't have anything that glitters," Randi

growled. "And I don't see why you want to look like him."

Max pulled a magazine out from under the mess on the bed.

"In this magazine there are many pictures of rock stars and their friends. And they are all wearing clothes that glitter."

Randi made a face. "That's Hollywood, Max. This is Riverside. And Chad Bellamy's not a rock *star*. He just plays in a band. I don't see what you're getting so worked up about."

Max gave Randi a look that suggested she was being very dense. "I am about to embark on the ultimate human experience," she said patiently. "I wish to be dressed appropriately."

Randi's frustration level rose three notches. "Max, you barely know the guy! And he's got a reputation, y'know. He could really hurt you!"

Max's eyebrows shot up. "Hurt me? I don't think he would try to do physical harm to me. Besides, I'm capable of defending myself."

A vision of Gary's cousin Ralph lying on the floor passed through Randi's mind. "Yes, I know," she said heavily. "But that's not the kind of hurt I'm talking about. That guy could break your heart!"

Finally her words were penetrating. Max actually looked thoughtful.

"Yes, I believe I understand what you mean. I saw something on a cover of a *Cosmopolitan*—"How to Recover from a Broken Heart." When I read that title, I must admit I was quite confused. I assumed that if one had a broken heart, one would have nothing to worry about, because one would be dead. But I realize now, the term is a figurative one. I suppose it was referring to the pain one feels when a love affair is unsuccessful. Am I correct?"

Randi smiled, a little sadly. "You got it."

"The pain of a broken heart," Max murmured pensively. "That is another kind of human feeling." Suddenly she brightened. "Then if, as you suggest, my relationship with Chad does not work out satisfactorily, I will have another human emotion to experience!" She leaned over and patted Randi's shoulder. "So you see, no matter what happens, I will have an interesting and educational human experience."

"Max," Randi moaned, "how can you be so . . . so logical about all this!"

Max replied with dignity. "It is in my nature. Perhaps, someday, if I learn to be more human, I will also become more illogical. However, I doubt that."

She hummed a popular song as she picked up her pocketbook and fumbled through her wallet. "I believe I have some baby-sitting money here. I will shop this afternoon for something with glitter."

Still humming, she grabbed her bathrobe and headed for the shower. Still shaking her head in wonderment and dismay, Randi dragged herself out of bed, slipped on her own robe, and padded down toward the kitchen.

She fixed herself some juice and cereal and sat down at the kitchen table. A few moments later her grandmother came in the room. As Randi looked up to greet her, her grandmother bent down and gave her an unusually hearty hug.

"Good morning, darling granddaughter," she purred.

Randi stared at her. "You're certainly in good spirits this morning."

Gramma beamed. "I have every right to be, and I have you to thank for it."

Randi suddenly figured out what she was talking about. "You mean—you and Officer Bronski—"

"No, we're not getting married, if that's what you're getting at," Gramma said hastily, "but he came over last night, we had a nice long heart-to-heart, and I believe we now have an understanding." She fixed herself a cup of tea and joined Randi at the table.

Randi gave her a warm smile. "I'm glad you guys worked it out, Gramma. And I'm glad *somebody's* taking my advice, for a change."

"What do you mean?" her grandmother asked, stirring her tea.

"I'm worried about Max," Randi confessed. She gave her grandmother a quick summary of the events leading to Max's date with Chad Bellamy.

"There's something about that guy I don't trust," she finished. "I know Max has come a long way, Gramma, but she's still so naive, she's so gullible. I just get bad feelings thinking about her being alone with him."

Her grandmother looked a little worried. "He's not dangerous, is he? He's not involved in alcohol, or drugs, is he?"

"Oh, no, nothing like that," Randi assured her. "At least, that's not what I've heard. But he's older—almost eighteen, I think—and I guess he's pretty sophisticated."

"And that worries you?"

"It's just that Max has this incredible hang-up about being in love with him, and I'll bet he's not the type to get serious. I just hate the thought of Max getting hurt."

Gramma smiled at her granddaughter fondly. "You care about Max a lot, don't you, Randi?"

Randi nodded. "I guess I always wanted a sister." She looked at her grandmother apprehensively. "Gramma, what do you think is going to happen when Mom and Dad get back? Do you think they'll let Max stay?"

"Well, they're certainly not going to throw her out," her grandmother replied comfortingly.

"But do you think we should tell them the truth about where Max comes from?"

Gramma fell silent. "I don't know, Randi," she said finally. "To tell you the truth, I have my doubts as to their believing that Max could actually have come from another planet." Then she shrugged and tried to look more cheerful. "I guess we'll just have to play it by ear. But don't worry about it—we'll think of a way to keep Max with us."

Randi smiled gratefully. "Thanks, Gramma."

"And don't worry about Max and this what's-his-name," her grandmother continued. "If he's not the right sort of boy for her, Max will learn that soon enough—and I think you're just going to have to let her make her own mistakes. By the way, how's everything going between you and Gary?"

"Huh? Oh, fine," Randi said vaguely. "I guess I've been so worried about Max, I haven't really been thinking about him a lot."

"Well, don't ignore him," Gramma admonished her. "Relationships take work, you know."

Randi grinned. "Are you telling me to practice what I preach?"

Gramma returned the smile. "Precisely."

Randi picked up her empty glass and bowl and carried them to the sink. "We're going out tonight, and it's the first time we'll be alone in ages," she said. "And I plan to give him my exclusive attention!"

Later that morning Max went off to go shopping for her glitter, and Randi, feeling terribly virtuous, stayed home and helped her grandmother clean house. Ellen stopped by for her at quarter of two to walk over to Desiree's together.

As they walked, Randi quickly brought Ellen up to date on current events.

"Wow, Chad actually asked her out," Ellen said dreamily. "Lucky Max."

"I wish I knew more about him," Randi said worriedly. "I've heard these rumors about him—you know, how he comes on to any girl he goes out with."

"That's probably just gossip," Ellen assured her. "Just because he plays in a band, everyone thinks he's wild. He's probably no different than any regular guy."

Randi wasn't convinced, but they had reached Desiree's house by then, so she didn't want to continue the discussion.

As they walked up the driveway to the door, she thought about how some houses actually reflected the people who lived in them. Her own house, with its faded shutters and bright, haphazardly planted flowers, always made her think of her grandmother— cozy and relaxed and easy to be around. And Desiree's house, with its cold, pale gray exterior, the impeccably neat lawn, and the ultramodern furniture inside which screamed "expensive"—all sort of showy, just like Desiree and her parents.

Mrs. Dupont answered the door. A mature version of Desiree, she always looked like she'd just returned from the beauty parlor.

"Well, hel-lo girls," she said in a phony-sweet way, "how lovely to see you! Come right in!"

She showed them into the impossibly neat living room, where six girls were perched on uncomfortable-looking chairs and sipping iced tea. As they greeted each other, Desiree, who was standing up, tapped her foot impatiently.

"You two are late," she snapped. Randi looked at her watch. "Only five minutes, Desiree," she said mildly.

"It's the principle of the thing," Desiree replied shortly. Randi just shrugged apologetically and took a seat next to Barbara Corelli. Desiree was obviously not in the greatest mood. Uneasily, she wondered if she had found out about Chad's date with Max.

"Where are the others?" Ellen asked curiously.

"Sandy and Lisa are still at camp," Karen Shulman told her. "And Connie's got a cold."

"I think Cherisse went away with her parents for the weekend," Christy Feeley offered.

Randi glanced at her curiously. "How was your date with Bubba last night?"

Christy giggled. "Oh, it was okay. But I met this other guy at the fair, from Madison High, and *really* cute, and he asked me for my phone number, and—"

Poor Bubba, Randi thought as Christy continued to prattle. Would he ever find a girl who could appreciate him?

"All *right*, girls," Desiree said authoritatively. "Could we *please* come to order? We've got a lot to talk about, and I've got to get ready for my date tonight."

"Are you going out with Chad?" Barbara asked. Desiree smiled condescendingly. "No, we broke up. I've got a date with someone else. Someone you don't know."

She didn't have a date, Randi decided. Otherwise she'd be telling them all about him. But at least she didn't seem to know about Chad having a date with Max. Otherwise, she'd be shooting dirty looks at Randi.

"First, we have to have our ritual," Desiree said. A

couple of girls groaned, and Desiree bristled. "Come *on*," she hissed, "join hands."

They all joined hands, and half-heartedly went through the ritual pledge.

> Star light, Star bright,
> We're Stars by day and Stars by night,
> We shine with beauty, we glow with pride,
> We're the Stars of Riverside.

> On my honor, I pledge undying loyalty and devotion to the Stars. I will never reveal the secrets of my sister Stars. And above all, I will never interfere with another Star's boyfriend.

When they finished with that, Desiree took over again. "Now we have to decide how we're going to expand this fall. According to my sources, there will be fifteen new junior girls transferring to Riverside High this fall."

"Who are her sources?" Randi whispered to Barbara.

"Her aunt's the secretary in the principal's office," Barbara whispered back. Desiree glared at her through narrowed eyes, and Barbara shrunk back into her chair.

"Now, I don't know if any of these girls are the type we want in the Stars," Desiree continued, "but if they are, you know the Dolls and the Alphas will be after them."

"What about the Debs?" Karen asked.

Desiree sneered. "If they're the type *we* want, they wouldn't be interested in the Debs. They're nerds."

"Hey, come on," Ellen objected. "Linda Fuller's a Deb, and I think she's pretty sharp."

Desiree turned her infamous glare on Ellen. "They're *nerds*," she repeated with conviction. "Anyway, my point is, we may have to do battle if we want to get any of these girls into the Stars."

"Like how?" Barbara asked.

"Like, we've got to show the new girls that we're the sharpest club at Riverside," Desiree stated. "We'll have to plan some really fantastic parties, with themes and all, to impress them."

"Hey, Randi," Karen said, "is Max going to be coming to Riverside this fall?"

Before Randi could answer her, Desiree jumped in. "You can forget about her," she snapped. "No way. She wouldn't fit in."

"Gee, I kind of like her," Barbara murmured mildly.

Desiree shook her head firmly. "She doesn't have Star quality."

Randi felt like she ought to say something like "If we don't take Max, I'll drop out." But she decided to hold off on pushing the issue. After all, she didn't even know for sure if Max *would* be going to school this fall, and even if she did, she wasn't sure Max would be classified as a junior. So she held her tongue—for the time being.

"We'll have our next meeting during the first week of school," Desiree said. "By then we should have all had a chance to look over the new girls. And I want every one of you to come up with some ideas for theme parties."

"Is that all?" Ellen asked.

"Yeah," Desiree replied. "We can't decide who we're going to run for class officers and all that till the others get back." Then she shrieked, "Matilda! We're ready for our refreshments!"

Randi couldn't believe it when a woman dressed in an actual maid's uniform came in with a trolley covered with pastries. Only someone as snobby as Desiree's mother would make the poor woman actually wear a dumb-looking frilly cap.

"Oh, goody," Ellen said happily, "now we can eat and gossip."

"Hey, Desiree," Christy said, "how come you and Chad broke up? He's soooo cute."

Desiree brushed aside a lock of hair and looked nonchalant. "Oh, he's cute enough, I guess," she said in a carefully casual voice. "But he got to be a drag. I mean, all he cares about is sex, sex, sex. And rock 'n' roll," she added, as an afterthought.

Randi almost choked on her eclair. "You mean," she sputtered, "he tried to . . . to . . . *you know* . . ."

Desiree gave her a look of pained superiority. "I didn't *let* him, of course. But that didn't stop him from trying. I got pretty tired of having to push him away."

"I'll bet she didn't push him all that much," Ellen whispered to Randi. Randi barely heard her. All she could think of was Max, alone in the car with Chad tonight.

"Of course, he *is* older," Desiree continued, with a look of sophisticated amusement on her face. "And I guess he expects more of a girl than just a good-night kiss." Then she sighed dramatically. "I'm still very fond of him, of course. But until he learns that I have a reputation to protect . . ."

Randi stopped listening. She was beginning to feel frantic. If Chad came on to Max, how would she respond? Would she think this was another 'human experience' she had to have? She got up from her chair.

"I've got to go," she said hurriedly. "Uh, I forgot, my grandmother needs me to run an errand." She hissed at Ellen, "I'll explain later," and dashed out.

She was out of breath by the time she ran in the door at home. "Max? Are you home?"

"She's in the bedroom," her grandmother replied, emerging from the kitchen. "What's wrong? You look upset."

"Oh, nothing," Randi said hastily. She didn't want to worry her grandmother about this. She managed a quick smile before she ran upstairs.

"How do you like this?" Max asked as Randi entered the bedroom.

Randi couldn't believe it. Max had gone all out in her attempt to look like a rock star's girlfriend. She was wearing Randi's plain black skirt, but she had hitched it up so it barely covered her thighs. The top was obviously new—black, and tight, with silver sequins. A black belt with silver studs was wrapped around her hips.

Definitely wild, and definitely sexy, Randi thought, her heart sinking. And definitely the kind of look that would turn on a guy like Chad.

Max was scrutinizing her expression. "Do you not think Chad will like this?" she asked anxiously.

"Oh, he'll like it all right," Randi said grimly. Then she bit her lower lip. She suddenly realized that she had no idea what to say to Max about Chad. If she told Max what Desiree had said, Max would ask a zillion questions—and Randi just didn't feel like she could give Max a satisfactory lecture on human morals, and what nice girls did and didn't do. Max probably wouldn't even understand. Or she'd think Randi was just trying to talk her out of dating Chad.

Max didn't seem to notice Randi's discomfort. She was too busy preening in front of the mirror.

"The saleslady said I should wear black lacy stockings with this," she said. "She told me that I would look very seductive. What does that mean, Randi?"

Randi started to groan, but suddenly she had an inspiration.

"Max," she said, "would you like me and Gary to double-date with you and Chad tonight?"

Max looked at her questioningly. "Double-date?"

"Like with you and Ralph," Randi explained. "The four of us would go out together."

Max frowned. "Would that be conducive to a romantic relationship?"

"Well, you see," Randi began, thinking quickly, "in this country, it's, uh, customary on first dates to, uh, double-date."

"Did you and Gary double-date on your first date?" Max asked.

"Well, no," Randi admitted, "but that was different, because, uh, we had known each other for so long. Look, Max, it would be fun, the four of us together. Okay?"

Max didn't look particularly convinced, but she said, "If you are certain that this is the custom . . ."

"Oh, it is, it is," Randi assured her hurriedly. "I'll go call Gary right now, okay?"

Max still looked doubtful, but she said okay, and Randi reached for the phone by her bed. But then she realized that she didn't want Max to hear the conversation, so she mumbled, "I have to get something in the kitchen," and ran downstairs.

Luckily her grandmother had disappeared, and Randi quickly dialed the number of the garage where Gary was working.

"Could I speak with Gary Morrison please?" As she waited she chewed on a fingernail. Gary wasn't going to like this idea. But after what she heard, there was no way she was going to let Max be alone with that . . . that lecher.

"Gary, hi, it's me."

He sounded surprised. "Is something wrong? You know I'm not supposed to get personal calls here."

"I know, and I'm sorry," Randi said quickly, "but

it's kind of important." She took a deep breath. "Gary, would you mind if we doubled tonight with Max and Chad?"

There was an uncomfortable silence on the other end, and Randi got to work on another fingernail.

"Yes, I would mind," Gary said finally. "I don't like Chad Bellamy. And I wanted to be alone with you. You said last night that you weren't going to do this anymore."

"I know," Randi said pleadingly, "but Gary, I'm so worried about Max. Desiree was talking about Chad today, and she practically said he's a sex maniac. I can't let Max be alone with him."

"First of all," Gary said irritably, "Desiree's probably exaggerating—she's famous for it. And secondly, Max can handle Chad if he comes on to her. You saw how she took care of Ralph."

"But she wasn't in love with Ralph," Randi argued. "If Chad tries something with her—there's no telling *what* she'll do!"

Gary sounded like he was ready to explode. "Are you ever going to stop trying to run her life? And start thinking about *us* for a change? I'm getting pretty sick of this, Randi."

You don't understand!" Randi practically shrieked. "She's not *like* us."

"What do you mean?"

Randi paused. She didn't want to go into Max's past on the phone. "I'll explain later. . . . Please, Gary, just for tonight, okay?"

There was another silence on the other end. Finally, Gary spoke. "Look, I've got to go."

"Is it okay, then?"

His voice was heavy. "I don't want to . . . "

"But will you?" she persisted.

He sounded strangely detached, almost cold.

"All right." And he hung up.

Randi replaced the receiver carefully and closed her eyes. She knew she should feel relieved, and she did— sort of.

But she didn't feel good.

# Chapter Eight

When she opened the door at eight, Randi tried to look as if nothing were wrong.

"Hi, Gary," she said, attempting a cheerful voice. "Gee, you look great."

He did, too. He was wearing a light sweater in a pale green that picked up the color of his eyes. She noticed for the first time that the sun had turned his normally sandy-colored hair almost blond. Only one thing was wrong with the way he looked. He wasn't smiling.

"Hi," he said, but his eyes wouldn't meet her's. Silently she let him in, and they went into the living room.

"Chad should be here soon," she said, in a voice she hoped sounded casual. "Max is still upstairs. She's been playing with makeup for hours, trying to prepare herself for this great romance she intends to have." She laughed lightly, hoping Gary would to the same. He didn't, but he finally looked directly at her. His eyes were serious.

"Randi," he said, "we need to talk tonight. I don't

care how, or when, or where, but we need some time alone."

"Sure, sure," Randi said hurriedly. "Uh, do you want anything? A soda, or something to eat?"

"No, thanks."

There was a strange, tense silence in the air. Suddenly Gary said, "You know, Randi, I had tickets for the baseball game in Madison tonight. For us. I had to give them to a friend."

Randi bit her lower lip. "Why didn't you tell me?"

"Would it have made any difference?"

Randi sighed. "I really need to stick with Max tonight. Like I told you—"

"Yeah, I know," Gary interrupted. "You've got to act like a watchdog for your little friend."

The way he expressed it really irritated her. "Speaking of my little friend, I guess I'd better go check on her," she said abruptly.

Gary laughed shortly. "Yeah, no telling what she might do without you watching her every minute."

Randi didn't bother to respond to this. She whirled around and went upstairs. She wasn't in the greatest mood to begin with, and his attitude was really beginning to get to her. Why couldn't he do this one little favor for her? Here she was, so worried about Max, and he wasn't even trying to understand. And to add to her general anxieties, there had been a telegram that afternoon—from her parents.

"Arriving home on Saturday. Eager to see you both."

Both—that meant Randi and Gramma. What would

they think when they discovered a new member of the family had arrived in their absence?

And now, with Gary acting like this—it was all she needed. She tried to be fair; after all, he didn't know the real reason Randi was so concerned about Max. Maybe once he knew, he'd be more understanding. She made a mental promise to tell him tonight—if they ever found themselves alone.

Max's eyes practically matched her new shirt—they glittered with anticipation.

"Has Chad arrived?"

"Not yet," Randi said. "What time did he say he'd be here?"

"Eight o'clock."

Randi glanced at the clock. "Well, it's almost eight-thirty now."

Max gave her a stricken look. "Do you think he has forgotten me?"

"No, no," Randi quickly assured her. "He'll probably be here any minute." The words had barely left her lips when she heard a car honking outside. She went to the window and looked out.

That flashy red sports car couldn't belong to anyone else but Chad Bellamy. Wasn't he planning to come to the door, Randi wondered. Obviously not, she decided when she heard another blast from the horn.

"Is he here?" Max asked excitedly.

"Yeah," Randi said unenthusiastically. "C'mon, let's go."

Gary was still in the living room, looking out the window at Chad's car.

"Isn't he coming to the door?" he asked.

"Guess not," Randi replied, without really looking at him. "Let's go outside."

Chad was actually getting out of the car as the three approached him. He eyed Max appreciatively, but all he said was, "Hey, what took you so long?"

"Hi, Chad," Randi said with false gaiety. "We thought we'd all go out together tonight."

Chad's expression clearly revealed that the idea didn't appeal to him any more than it had to Gary.

"Randi said it was customary to date in pairs," Max added, and gave him a sidelong smile. She had apparently figured out what the word *seductive* meant.

Chad scowled and indicated his car. "Four people won't fit in here."

He was right—the car was a two-seater.

"We can take Gary's car," Randi said brightly.

"Or we can go in separate cars," Gary said. It was the first thing he had said since they'd gone outside. Randi glared at him. That was the last thing she wanted. No way was she going to give Chad the opportunity to be alone in a car with Max.

She spoke through clenched teeth. "Oh, I think it would be much more fun to go together in one car."

Chad shrugged, and then he grinned at Max. "Okay. . . . At least *we* get the backseat."

And I'm going to keep my eye on you, Randi added mentally. She glanced at Max. She was still smiling at Chad in that sexy way. She wondered if Max had any idea what Chad was implying.

They all piled into Gary's car.

"Where are we going, anyway?" Gary asked.

"I got passes to the new disco in Madison," Chad replied. "It's supposed to be really hot."

Randi turned and gave him a look of alarm. "But that's an adult club. Don't you have to be twenty-one to get in?"

Chad smiled confidently. "Don't worry about that. I've got connections."

Randi glanced at Gary. His face was set in a totally unreadable expression. All he said was, "How do we get there?"

Chad gave him directions, and they set off. There were a few moments of silence, and then Randi heard Chad saying something to Max. His voice was low, so she had to strain to hear every word.

"You're looking pretty hot tonight yourself," he murmured.

"I don't *feel* hot," Max replied. "There's a nice breeze tonight."

Randi heard Chad laugh softly. "I really dig your hair. I'm into the whole punk scene, too."

"Yes, punk is a very interesting phenomenon," Max said. "Although it originated as a political statement in England, it has developed into a musical format which extends the concept of new wave."

She sounded like she had memorized an entire article on punk music.

"Yeah, we play punk, new wave, disco, all that stuff," Chad was saying. "You don't look like you're from around here. Where are you from—New York?"

Randi jumped into the conversation. "Max doesn't

111

know where she's from, Chad. Isn't that interesting? She's got amnesia."

"Oh, yeah?" He sounded intrigued. "Wow, that's real kinky." He paused, and added, "I guess you've got a lot to learn." His voice became lower, more intimate. "And I just might be the best teacher."

Randi decided Chad and Gary's awful cousin Ralph must have read the same book: "How to come on to an amnesiac." She didn't like the eager way that Max responded.

"Oh, yes, I have much to learn. About life and . . . "

Oh, don't say it, Randi thought frantically. But she did. " . . . and love."

Randi turned her head slightly just in time to see Chad edge closer to Max and toss an arm casually over her shoulder. "Sounds good to me."

Randi tried to catch Gary's eye so she could give him a meaningful "you see what I mean" look. But his eyes were fixed on the road. So she turned and faced Chad and Max, who, at this point, were looking deeply into each other's eyes and not saying a word. She tried to think of a conversation-starter.

"The band sounded great the other night at the Teen Scene," she said.

Chad responded without taking his eyes off Max. "Yeah, thanks."

"Are you still playing there?" she persisted.

It seemed to take a major effort on Chad's part to reply. "Nah, that gig's finished. I don't think we'll be playing there that much anymore. The money's lousy, and it's small-time stuff anyway."

"Where are you playing next?" Randi asked. She didn't really care, but she wanted to keep Chad talking.

"We got an audition next week at this joint we're going to now, the Ritz. This could be our big break. Record company people show up there sometimes."

Max seemed interested in this. "Then you could be discovered, and cut a record, and become a big rock star."

Modesty was apparently not one of Chad's major virtues. "Yeah, that's what we figure. Cut an album, go on tour, make it big. I figure, give Spit a year, and we'll be on the cover of *Rolling Stone*."

Gary finally spoke, but all he said was, "Is this where we turn off?"

Chad managed to take his eyes of Max just long enough to glance out the window. "Yeah . . . make a left here, and it's the second right."

The low, sprawling building they pulled up to had black windows and a huge neon sign: THE RITZ. And under that, in just slightly smaller letters: WHERE THE ELITE MEET. Randi saw several people going in, and they looked very sophisticated.

"Are you sure we're going to be able to get in, Chad?" she asked nervously. She had a sudden image of all four of them being arrested for being underage.

"No sweat," Chad said easily, jumping out of the car. As they approached the night club, Randi saw a couple walk, or rather, stagger out. They were both giggling like hyenas. Randi clutched Gary's arm.

"Gary, do you think this place is okay?"

"No, I don't," he replied firmly. "And I don't think we belong here. Let's go someplace else."

But Chad had already reached the door, and with mock gallantry he held it open for the rest of them. Max strolled right on in.

"We'll just stay a little while," Randi whispered to Gary. "And then maybe we can talk them into leaving."

Gary seemed about to object, but Randi looked at him pleadingly. "Ten minutes," he muttered, and they followed Max in.

If Randi had thought the Teen Scene was impressive, she was totally unprepared for the glitz of the Ritz. The entire place seemed to be covered with glitter. There was a huge silvery dance floor, and overhead colored lights pulsated and rotated, giving the whole scene a surrealistic look.

And the people—at least the ones Randi could see in the dim lights—looked like the people in Max's rock magazines. Women with pink crew cuts, men with blue mohawks—actually, Randi wasn't even sure which were men and which were women. A man dressed entirely in leather who stood at the door looked like he was about to stop them, but Chad showed him some passes, and he waved them on.

"Let's get some drinks," Chad said, and led them to the bar. "Gimme a beer," he said to the bartender, and turned to the rest of them. "What are you guys drinking?"

"I'll just have a ginger ale," Randi said.

"Nothing for me," Gary said.

Chad looked pained. "Hey, c'mon, you guys, they know me here, it's okay. Have a real drink."

"No, thanks," Gary said shortly.

"How about you, Max?" Chad said. "You'll have a beer with me, right?"

Max looked interested. "I've never had a beer. . . ."

"And you're not going to have one now," Randi said firmly. "Don't try to get her to drink, Chad."

He gave her a sour look. "Since when do *you* give the orders around here?"

Happily, Max intervened. "Perhaps Randi is right. I don't want *too* many new experences in one night. I'll have a ginger ale, too."

Chad grimaced, but he complied with their orders. He gulped down his beer, and then grabbed Max's arm. "Let's dance."

Randi looked at Gary, but he shook his head before she could even ask. "No, I don't feel like dancing."

They stood there awkwardly, not speaking.

"Hey, doll, I'll dance with you." The voice came from a big, burly man in a leather jacket. He was grinning at Randi in a way that gave her the creeps.

"No, thank you," she said politely.

"Aw, c'mon baby," the man said, and reached out as if to grab her arm.

Gary took Randi's hand and faced the man squarely. "Beat it!" he said.

The man gave Gary a threatening look. "I wasn't talking to you, buddy. It's your foxy chick I want."

Randi looked at Gary. His face hardened. "C'mon, we're getting out of here," he said firmly. He pulled Randi away from the man and toward the door.

Finally Randi had to agree with him. "But I can't leave Max here," she said.

"So go get her," Gary said. "But we're getting out of here—*now*."

Randi searched for Max in the dancing crowd. Usually she could spot Max anywhere—but in this crowd, she wasn't quite so distinctive. Finally she spotted Max and Chad dancing, and she waved to them wildly. Max waved back cheerfully.

Randi pushed her way through the crowd toward them. "Max," she said urgently, "Gary wants to leave."

"Then he can leave," Chad said.

Randi ignored him. "Max, you've got to come with us. This isn't a nice place."

Max looked bewildered, and Chad sneered. "Hey, little Miss Goody Two-Shoes can't handle the big time."

Randi sneered right back. "If this is the big time, I'll take the small time, thank you." It wasn't a very sharp retort, but it was the best she could do under the circumstances. "Max, come on."

"Don't go," Chad said, in a voice that reeked of phony sincerity. "I want you to stay here . . . with me."

Max looked first at Chad, then at Randi. "Randi," she said, "you know it is rude to leave a date. I read that in *Seventeen*."

116

"Max!"

"Bug off," Chad barked. "Leave me and my chick alone, okay?"

"I want to stay here with Chad," Max said plaintively. "We have had our double date. Now we can be alone with our boyfriends."

Randi was at a loss for words. Just then Gary appeared by her side, and he took her arm, almost roughly. "C'mon, we're leaving."

"But how will Chad and Max get home?" she asked wildly.

"Don't worry about us," Chad muttered. "I've got friends here. We'll get a ride."

Before Randi could say another word, Gary pulled her off the dance floor.

"Hey!" Randi practically yelled. "Don't pull me like that!" But Gary ignored her and held on to her arm until they reached the car.

"Gary, I can't leave Max in a place like that!"

Gary didn't say a word. He held the car door open for her, and Randi reluctantly got in. He went around to the other side and got in, but he didn't start the car immediately.

"Gary," Randi repeated, "I can't just leave her!"

Gary looked at her oddly, and when he spoke, his voice was cold as ice. "I can't believe you're that worried about Max. In fact, I think I've just about figured this whole thing out."

Randi looked at him blankly. "What do you mean?"

"I don't think you care about us at all. I think you've just been using me, to take you places, play 'boyfriend' for you. That's all Desiree wanted, too. And now that I've had some experience with girls like you, I'm not about to get caught in a trap like that again."

Randi couldn't believe she was hearing this. "Are you crazy? I'm not like Desiree. Gary, I *love* you."

He laughed, but it wasn't a happy laugh. "You've got a funny way of showing it." He started the car and then pulled out of the parking lot.

Randi tried to collect her thoughts.

"Gary," she said tensely, "I'm going to tell you the real reason I'm so worried about Max. I'm going to tell you the truth about her."

Gary didn't say anything. He had his eyes on the road they were going down.

Randi took a deep breath. "Remember that day you saw us on the bleachers in back of the high school? And Max had on that funny black outfit?"

Gary wouldn't look at her, but at least he spoke. "I didn't notice what she was wearing."

"Well, that outfit—it was sort of like a uniform. It's what everyone wears, where she comes from." She paused and took another deep breath. "Max doesn't have amnesia, Gary. That's just what we tell everyone. Max comes from another planet. She beamed down to Earth."

For a moment Gary didn't say anything. Then he uttered a short laugh. "That's a great story, Randi. You must have even less respect for me than I thought."

"But it's *true!*" Randi exclaimed. "You have to

118

believe me. That's why I get so protective. She doesn't understand anything about Earth, or the way humans act, or anything."

"So Max isn't a human being," Gary said sarcastically. "Gee, she does a great impersonation."

"Gary, just listen to me—"

But he wouldn't. "Look, Randi, when you feel like being straight with me, we can talk. Right now I don't feel like hearing any more of your fairy tales."

Now Randi was getting angry. She had a feeling that if she kept on talking, if she provided more details, she could make Gary believe her. But she was wondering if it was worth it. If he really cared about her, he'd be listening to her, he'd believe her. And she had thought he was such a sensitive person. What a joke.

"Oh, forget it," she snapped. "I should have known better than to have thought you'd understand. I guess you're not the person I thought you were."

"Funny," Gary said, "I was just thinking the same thing."

They were silent the rest of the way. Randi was in a daze, still not believing what was happening. She just wanted to be home, and alone with her thoughts.

And then they were there, in front of her house. Gary moved to get out of the car, but Randi just muttered, "Don't bother," and opened her own door. As she got out, Gary spoke.

"If you ever feel like telling me the truth . . ."

"Forget it," Randi said sharply, and slammed the door.

Once inside the house she leaned against the door

and tried to figure out what had just happened. But her thoughts were totally incoherent. She only knew that she was absolutely furious.

She went up to her room. The house was silent—her grandmother must have gone out with Officer Bronski.

She threw herself on her bed and pounded the pillow. *Why* wouldn't he believe her? How could he be so incredibly insensitive? How could she have been so wrong about him? Tears of anger and frustration filled her eyes.

Finally there were no more tears left. She pulled herself off the bed and went to the bathroom to wash her face. She wanted to go to bed, but she was still worried about Max, and she felt like she had to wait up for her.

She went down to the den, switched on the television, and stared at a late movie without even seeing it. She must have dozed off, because suddenly she opened her eyes and there was something else on the screen. And then she heard the front door open.

She went upstairs and was relieved to see Max there, intact.

"Are you okay?" she asked anxiously. "What happened after we left?"

Max looked very tired. "Nothing happened. We danced for a short time, and then Chad didn't feel very well. We saw some friends of his, and they took us home. Chad fell asleep in the car."

Randi followed her up to the bedroom.

"Did you have a good time?"

"I'm not sure," Max replied sleepily. "Perhaps if I

describe it to you more completely in the morning, you can tell me if I had a good time." Then she looked at Randi. "You don't look well. Did you not have a good time?"

Randi shook her head. "Gary and I had a fight. I guess we broke up. I really don't much feel like talking about it right now."

Max scrutinized her face. "Are you feeling hurt? Do you have a broken heart?"

Randi managed a wan smile. "Yeah, I guess so."

Max picked up a magazine lying on her bed. "Would this help?"

Randi glanced at the *Cosmopolitan* cover. "How to Mend a Broken Heart," she read aloud. "No, Max, I don't think it will help."

# Chapter Nine

When Randi woke up the next morning, the pillow under her head was still damp from her tears. She lay there for a few moments, feeling totally dismal. The greatest romance of her life was over. It was pure tragedy.

All right, they had only dated for three weeks—but they were three wonderful weeks. Did the end of a three-week romance constitute a tragedy? How many weeks did Romeo and Juliet have?

Now, don't start feeling sorry for yourself, she told herself fiercely; people make mistakes, and Randi, you made a big one. But at least you know you didn't lie to him, and if he refuses to believe you, that's *his* problem. At least you've still got your pride.

But as much as she resisted the thought, she couldn't help but see his side, too. She *could* have explained about Max to him sooner, before the tensions had started to build. But it was too late to think about that now.

She eased herself out of bed and glanced at Max, still sleeping peacefully. As well she might—after all, icky as Chad might be, she now had a boyfriend.

The smell of bacon cooking drifted upstairs, and Randi, to her surprise, realized she was actually hungry. She slipped into her robe and went down to the kitchen.

"How come you're cooking bacon?" she asked curiously. "I thought you swore off meat." She clearly remembered the day Max had explained how she never ate anything that had ever been "sentient"—capable of feeling. And how her grandmother had enthusiastically accepted that notion for herself.

Her grandmother looked a little abashed. "I missed it," she confessed. "And Carl is such a meat-and-potatoes man—I got tired of munching salads while he devoured a juicy steak.

"Besides," she continued as she beat some eggs, "if Max is going to be living with us permanently, she'll have to get used to meat in the house, even if she doesn't eat it herself. And your parents have enough in the way of surprises waiting for them here without having to accept a new vegetarian diet, too."

Randi was relieved to hear this. Although her grandmother had become pretty creative with vegetarian cooking, Randi had been getting pretty tired of meat-free meals herself.

"Did Max have a good time on her date last night?" Gramma asked.

"I don't know," Randi said. "We haven't really

talked about it yet. She got in after me, and . . . and I guess I was pretty sleepy."

Something in her voice caught her grandmother's attention, and she turned to Randi with a look of concern.

"And how about you? Did *you* have a good time last night?"

Randi was all prepared to say "Oh, sure, fine," but she never was a very good liar. "No," she said bluntly. "Gary and I broke up."

"Oh, honey, I'm so sorry." Quickly Gramma began to pile bacon and eggs on two plates and put them on the kitchen table. "Let's eat, and you can tell me all about it—if you want to, that is."

"Okay," Randi said, and sat down. She eyed the food hungrily. "Gee, I thought having a broken heart made a person not eat much. But I'm starving."

"You're just like me," Gramma said comfortingly. "When I'm miserable, I'm ravenous. Now, tell me what happened."

Randi went through the whole story—how she'd been worried about Max, especially in regard to Chad, how Gary had been getting annoyed, how they'd gone to the disco and how Gary wouldn't believe her when she told him the truth about Max.

"So it's all over," she concluded, trying to sound firm and confident. "I'm not going to beg him to believe me."

Her grandmother looked thoughtful. "Poor Gary," she said.

"Poor Gary!" Randi exclaimed. "What about poor me? I'm the one who's not being trusted!"

"Think about this, Randi," Gramma said slowly. "What if you were told, out of nowhere, that someone you knew was from another planet? How would you respond?"

Randi thought about it. "It would depend," she said finally, "on who was telling me. If it was someone I trusted—"

"Oh, come now," her grandmother remonstrated. "*Think* about it, Randi. Gary's a down-to-earth, practical person. He's beginning to feel you don't care about him—and let's face it, you *haven't* been giving him too much in the way of undivided attention lately. And then, out of the blue, you tell him Max is from another planet."

"But *you* believed it," Randi argued, "and so did Ellen when I told her."

"But I'm not a down-to-earth practical person," her grandmother replied. "And neither is Ellen. *You* are, though. How did *you* react when Max told you about herself?"

"I didn't believe her," Randi admitted. "But Gary should have believed me!" she burst out. "I'm supposed to be his girlfriend!"

"But you haven't really known each other that long," her grandmother reminded her. "You know, when Carl Bronski was upset about all my activities, it was because he didn't really understand the kind of person I am. We talked it out, and now he knows me better, and he understands more. Maybe if you talk with Gary . . ."

"I'm *not* going to plead with him to understand," Randi said hotly. "I have *some* pride left."

Her grandmother smiled. "There's that word again—*pride*. Remember when you said that pride could kill a relationship?"

"This is different," Randi muttered. Just then she heard Max coming out of the bedroom upstairs. "Gramma," she said quickly, "Max knows Gary and I broke up, but she doesn't know why. Don't tell her, okay? She might feel like it's her fault."

Her grandmother nodded understandingly just as Max came in the room. She looked a little paler than usual that morning, and her nose wrinkled at the sight of the bacon.

"That was a living creature," she said pointedly.

Her grandmother laughed. "I know, Max. But I'm afraid we're just a culturally carnivorous people, and you'll have to get used to that if you're going to stay with us permanently."

Max didn't reply; she simply shook her head with obvious disapproval.

Gramma rose from her chair. "I'm planning to go to the mall today. Would you girls like to come along? I'm in the mood to look at the new fall clothes, and I just might be willing to buy them for someone else."

Randi knew her grandmother was trying to cheer her up. But she just wasn't in the mood to look at new clothes. They'd only remind her of the school dances she *wouldn't* be going to with Gary.

"No thanks, Gramma," she said. "I think I'll just stay home today."

"I will go with you," Max said. "Now that I have a boyfriend, I will need more clothes."

She didn't sound particularly enthusiastic, though, and Randi shot her a curious look as Gramma left the room.

"Didn't you have a good time with Chad last night?" she asked.

Briefly Max repeated what she had said the night before—they danced, and Chad fell asleep on the way home.

"We have another date tonight." There was a brief second of silence before she added, "He wants to teach me all about love."

Randi gasped. Did Max have any idea what that could possibly mean?

"Max," she said tentatively, "you know . . . I mean . . . there are, well, things men and women do that, uh, maybe you're not ready to do . . . I mean . . ."

Max looked at her questioningly. "I don't understand."

Randi took a deep breath. "Making love," she said weakly.

Max's expression didn't change.

*"Physical* love," Randi said.

Max stared at her. Then her expression reflected comprehension.

"Ah! You are referring to sexual intercourse."

Randi gulped. "Uh, yeah."

Max looked at her as if she weren't very bright. "I

127

have no intention of engaging in sexual intercourse. Why would you think that? I don't wish to bear a child at this time."

Randi breathed a sigh of relief. She decided this wasn't the time to tell Max that humans didn't make love only to have children. "That's good," was all she said.

"Now I must dress to go shopping," Max said. "Why aren't you coming with us?"

"Oh, I have things to do," Randi said vaguely. Max didn't seem very satisfied with that answer, but she didn't press the question.

Later, after Max and Gramma left, Randi almost wished she *had* gone with them. Alone in the house, she was feeling even more depressed. She tried to read, but she couldn't concentrate. She turned on the TV, but there was nothing to watch. She kept listening for the phone, but it didn't ring. Was Gary missing her at all? Obviously not, or he'd call to apologize.

But just as she was listlessly flipping through a magazine, the phone *did* ring, and she leaped up. She reached it before the first ring had finished, took a deep breath, and let it ring twice more before she picked it up and calmly, nonchalantly said, "Hello?"

Her heart sank when she heard the voice on the other end.

"Hi, Randi? It's Bubba."

She tried not to sound too disappointed when she replied, "Hi, Bubba. What are you up to?"

"Not much," the voice on the other end said. "What about you?"

"I'm just sitting around," Randi said. "Gramma and Max went out shopping." Suddenly she felt the need for some companionship. "Wanna come over?"

"Okay. See you in a minute."

As she hung up the phone Randi felt a little more cheerful. She hadn't seen much of Bubba lately. She'd known him since they were little kids, and they used to practically live at each other's houses. He had had a big crush on Max when she first appeared earlier that month, and they had gone out a few times. But then Max had decided she had no more need for him—and she had only been using him to find out what the dating experience was like. Ever since then Bubba had been a little distant.

He was on Randi's doorstep in less than a minute—which was not surprising, given the fact that he lived right next door.

"Hungry?" Randi asked. It was an unnecessary question. Bubba was *always* hungry.

"Whatcha got?" Bubba asked, following her into the kitchen.

"How about potato chips, onion dip, chocolate chip cookies, and lemonade?"

"Sounds good to me," Bubba said happily, and Randi got the stuff out.

They settled with their goodies in the den, and Randi put some music on the stereo.

"Are you seeing Christy Feeley now?" Randi asked. She remembered the way Christy had spoken of Bubba at Desiree's, but she hoped maybe she had changed her mind.

"Nah," Bubba said between mouthfuls of chips. "She's kind of a dip, you know what I mean? I can't stand the way she's always giggling."

"Yeah, I know what you mean," Randi said. She knew she wasn't supposed to say anything negative about a sister Star in front of anyone else, but with Bubba, she knew from experience that anything they said to each other was strictly confidential. "I couldn't figure out what you were doing with her at the carnival anyway."

"Well, I had to take *someone*," Bubba said. "Of course, I would've rather been with Max. Who was she with that night, anyway?"

"No one," Randi replied. "She just came along with me and Gary."

"Oh, yeah, you've been dating Gary Morrison," Bubba said. "How's that going?"

Randi didn't want to go into the whole story. "Okay," she said, and hoped he wouldn't ask anything more.

Luckily he had other things on his mind. He sighed deeply.

"I still think about Max all the time," he said sadly. "Randi, do you think there's any chance in the world we might get together?"

"I don't know," Randi replied honestly. "Max is . . . unusual, Bubba." She had to remind herself that Bubba didn't know the truth about Max. He still thought she was an ordinary girl who happened to have amnesia.

Bubba sighed again. "I can't even get interested in

another girl," he said. "Has she been going out with anyone else?"

Randi figured she'd better be straight with him. "Sort of," she admitted. "She went out with Chad Bellamy last night."

"Chad Bellamy?!"

Randi was surprised that he seemed so startled. "Well, yeah. They met, and . . . he broke up with Desiree, you know."

Bubba looked perplexed. "Since when? This morning?"

Now it was Randi's turn to look puzzled. "No . . . the night we saw you at the carnival. They had a big fight."

Bubba still looked confused. "But I saw them together last night."

"What are you talking about? Gary and I were with Max and Chad last night."

Bubba shook his head. "I was with a bunch of guys at the coffee shop. . . . You know, that all-night one on Main Street? It was real late, about two in the morning. We'd been bowling. Chad and Desiree were in the booth across from us." He coughed and added delicately, "They didn't come in there to eat, if you know what I mean."

Randi's mouth fell open. Max had gotten in just around twelve-thirty.

"I can't believe it," she murmured.

"If they had a fight, they were definitely making up," Bubba asserted. "I hope Max isn't too interested in him."

"She's supposed to have a date with him tonight," she said.

Bubba looked concerned. "Well, he and Desiree looked like they were going at it pretty heavy last night. Gee, I hope Max isn't too hung up on him."

Randi looked at him affectionately. Here Max had shot him down, and he was still worried that she might get hurt. What a nice guy. . . . But what was going on here? Had Chad and Desiree gotten back together?

"I'm going to call Ellen," she said suddenly. "She'll know what's going on."

She ran up to the kitchen and dialed Ellen's number. Luckily she was home.

"Ellen," she asked hurriedly, "do you know anything about Chad and Desiree? Did they get back together?"

"No kidding!" Ellen exclaimed. "How'd you find out so fast? It's unbelievable, isn't it? I thought it was all over between them! But then I talked to Barbara this morning, and she said that Karen said that—"

"Ellen, c'mon," Randi interrupted, "get to the point!"

"Supposedly he called Desiree at one in the morning! Can you believe it?! Luckily she has her own phone. Gee, I wish my parents would let me have my own phone—"

"Ellen!"

"Okay, okay. Anyway, he called her, and she snuck out of the house, and he picked her up, and they went to some coffee shop. Boy, if I ever did something like that, my parents would just about kill me—"

"Ellen," Randi interrupted again. "Just tell me—did they get back together?"

"Well," Ellen said, "according to Barbara, Karen said that Amy's brother saw them at the coffee shop, and they looked like they were *definitely* together, if you know what I mean." Then she gasped. "Wow—how's Max going to feel about this? Is she still hung up on him?"

"Ellen," Randi said in a rush, "I've got to go. I'll talk to you later." She hung up the phone and stood there, frozen. Poor Max! How was she going to feel?

She remembered Bubba back down in the den and slowly made her way back there. He looked up inquisitively.

"What did Ellen say?"

"You were right," Randi said slowly. "They *did* get back together."

Bubba was silent. Finally he said, "Do you think Max is going to be very hurt?"

"I don't know," Randi murmured. "What I'm wondering is . . . should I tell her?"

Bubba looked thoughtful. "Are you absolutely, positively sure that Chad and Desiree are back together?"

"Well, Ellen said that Barbara said that Karen said . . ."

"I get it," Bubba said. "Look, they might have had another fight before the evening was over. You said Chad has a date with Max tonight, right?"

"Yeah, that's what she told me."

Bubba shrugged. "Well, if he and Desiree are back

133

together, he'll have to break the date, right? So why don't you just wait and see what happens?"

"I guess you're right," Randi said sadly. "Oh, poor Max. I just don't want her to be hurt. This is exactly what I was afraid would happen. I knew that Chad Bellamy was no good."

"Yeah," Bubba said heavily, and got up. "I'll never understand why you girls always go for the heart-breakers."

How true, Randi thought. She walked Bubba to the door, where he turned to her.

"Look, Randi, about Max—"

"Yes?"

He smiled, a little sadly. "If she needs anyone to pick up the pieces, if you know what I mean . . ."

Randi returned the smile. "Yeah, Bubba. I hear you."

After he left, she continued to sit there, staring into space. Poor Max, she thought. And poor me. Well, at least we'll have each other for comfort. And now she'll know all about broken hearts. . . .

Only a few minutes later Gramma and Max came home. They were both loaded with bags and packages.

"Wow," Randi said, hoping her voice sounded normal. "You guys must have bought out the stores."

"They're all mine," Gramma said gaily. "I fell in love with everything I saw! But Max didn't see anything she liked."

Randi looked at Max. She just shrugged. And then the phone rang. Gramma was the first to reach it.

"Max, it's for you," she said, and smiled. "It's a

boy." She handed the phone to Max and turned to Randi. "I left some things in the car. I'll be right back."

Randi bit her lip. Was her friend about to have her heart broken?

Max spoke into the phone. "Hello?" There was a moment of silence, and then she said, "Yes. I understand. Good-bye."

And she hung up the phone.

Randi watched her carefully. "Was that Chad?"

Max nodded.

"What did he say?"

Max spoke carefully. "He said that he and Desiree have . . . How did he put it? They have 'made up.' He will not be taking me out for a date tonight."

At least he had the decency to tell the truth, Randi thought. "Oh, Max," she said compassionately, "I'm so sorry."

Max sat down. She didn't speak, and she stared at nothing.

"Max? Are you okay?"

Max spoke calmly. "I am waiting."

"Waiting for what?"

"The feeling of heartbreak."

Randi waited with her in silence. Finally she asked, "Are you feeling it yet?"

Max looked perturbed. "I'm not sure. What is it supposed to feel like?"

Randi tried to describe her own feelings. "Sort of sad, and, I don't know, just empty. Do you feel like crying?"

135

Max shook her head.

"Then I guess you don't have a broken heart."

"Which means," Max said slowly, "that I never really loved him."

Randi sighed in relief. "That's probably true."

Max sighed, too—but it wasn't in relief. "I should have loved him," she said sadly. "But perhaps I'm not capable of loving. Maybe I'm just—not human enough."

"Oh, Max—" Randi started to protest, but Max wasn't listening. She rose stiffly from her chair and walked over to the window, her back to Randi.

Randi watched her silently. There she goes, she thought to herself—the only girl in the world who's miserable because her heart *isn't* broken.

# Chapter Ten

"I'm back," Gramma said as she came into the living room, her arms full of more bags. The cheeriness in her voice faded as she took in the two long faces that greeted her.

"Good grief," she said, looking first at Randi, then at Max. "Randi, your gloom must be contagious. What's going on?"

Max didn't even seem to hear her, so Randi answered. "Chad broke the date tonight with Max."

Her grandmother turned a sympathetic eye on Max. "I'm sorry, dear. I know you had quite a crush on him . . ."

Max stood up abruptly. "I have to think about this. Please excuse me." She left the room and went upstairs.

"She must feel very hurt," Gramma said, looking after her.

"Mmm," Randi murmured. She wondered if she should explain that Max was upset because she *didn't* care about Chad, not because she *did*. Then she realized that her grandmother was still standing there with bags in her arms, and she jumped up to help her.

"What's all this?" she asked as they brought the bags into the kitchen.

"Food, and lots of it," Gramma replied. "Carl's coming for dinner, and I'm afraid I bought way too much." Then, too casually, she added, "Perhaps we should invite someone else to join us."

"Like who?"

Gramma looked thoughtful. "How about Gary?"

Randi looked at her as if she were crazy. "Are you kidding? I told you—it's over between us."

"Now, you listen to me, young lady," her grandmother said firmly. "I'm going to give you a little of your own advice. You're miserable, and I'll bet Gary's miserable, too. I think you should call him right this minute and invite him over for dinner. What have you got to lose?"

Randi opened her mouth to reply, but her grandmother wouldn't let her. "And don't you dare tell me 'pride.' It was pride that kept me from calling Carl Bronski, and pride that made me unhappy. Now, there's not much I can do to help Max right now, but I absolutely refuse to have *two* miserable girls in the house. You get on that phone right now and *call him!*"

Randi stared at her grandmother. "But what would I say? I am *not* going to apologize to him."

"Who said anything about apologizing? Just call and ask him over for dinner." Then she smiled. "And maybe Carl and I will take Max with us to a movie after dinner. Then you two can have the house all to yourselves." Her eyes twinkled. "But don't do anything I wouldn't do!"

Randi had to smile at that. Maybe her grandmother was right—maybe she should call him. After all, she couldn't feel any worse than she did right now. If Gary said no, she'd be miserable—but she was miserable anyway, so what difference would it make?

But she still had her doubts. "I wish he'd call me first," she murmured.

"This is the twentieth century," her grandmother replied firmly. "Women don't have to wait for men to call! Tell me this—do you really want to get back together with Gary?"

Randi nodded.

"Then call him!" Gramma ordered. "Take charge of your own life! Take matters into your own hands!"

Randi looked at her grandmother admiringly. "You're really something, Gramma."

The older woman looked at the clock. "Tell him dinner will be ready in two hours." Then, with a wink, she sailed out of the room.

Randi looked at the phone apprehensively. She bit her lip. She chewed on her last remaining fingernail. She twisted a lock of hair. And then, hands trembling, she picked up the receiver and dialed.

"Gary? Hi, it's me."

There was a moment of silence before she heard, "Hi, Randi."

Randi gripped the phone tightly. "Would you like to come over for dinner?"

Again there was a silence. "Now?"

"Yeah. Well, dinner's not for another couple of hours. But if you come now, we could—talk."

"Okay."

Randi was afraid to believe her own ears. "Did you say—okay?"

"Yeah."

"Well," Randi said lamely, "I'll, uh, see you then."

"Right." And he hung up.

Slowly Randi replaced the receiver. She felt like the room was spinning. Could a person go from total despair to complete elation in ten seconds? Obviously!

"Gramma!" she shrieked. "Max!"

Within a matter of seconds both came running into the kitchen. "What happened?" her grandmother asked anxiously. Even Max's vacant expression reflected concern.

"He's coming!" Randi exclaimed joyously. "He said yes!" Then she realized she was wearing her grungiest jeans. "I have to change! Max, come help me!"

She paused before racing out of the room to give her grandmother a hug. "Thanks, Gramma," she whispered. "I just wish we could do something for Max."

"I'll think about it," her grandmother promised.

Max followed Randi to the bedroom.

"Now, what should I wear?" Randi asked, fumbling through her closet. "I don't want to look too dressed up, but I've got to look good."

"How about this?" Max asked listlessly, offering her glitter shirt.

Randi shook her head. "No, Gary's not into glitter

140

like Chad." Then she turned to her. "Oh, Max, I'm sorry. I know you're hurting, and here I am acting all giddy and crazy."

"Because you're in love," Max said glumly.

Randi nodded. "And you will be, too, someday. Just because it didn't work out with Chad—well, you'll feel this way about someone someday, really you will." She grabbed a clean pair of jeans and pulled them on.

Max shook her head. "No, Randi, I don't think so. It's true that I'm part human. But I don't think that I'm human enough to love."

Randi was about to argue this, but then she heard the doorbell. "He's here!" she gasped. "Oh, Max, wish me luck." She ran a brush through her hair and dashed downstairs. Her grandmother had let Gary in, and they were sitting in the living room.

As soon as Randi entered her grandmother stood up. "I think I'll see about getting dinner started," she said, winking at Randi as she left the room.

Alone with Gary, Randi didn't know what to say. And then, at the exact same time, they both said, "I'm sorry about last night—" and stopped. They stared at each other for a second, and then they both started laughing.

"Oh, Gary," Randi said, hoping she wouldn't embarrass herself by bursting into tears of happiness. "I know I've been taking you for granted. I was thinking about Max, and I wasn't thinking about you . . ."

"No, it's my fault," Gary insisted. "I wanted *all* your attention, and I shouldn't have been so selfish. And last night—well, I can't stand that Chad Bellamy,

141

and then when you hit me with that crazy story you made up about Max . . ."

Randi stopped smiling. "But I didn't make it up."

Gary's smile faded, too. "Oh, come on, Randi, I know you were putting me on. You don't expect me to believe—" He stopped talking suddenly, and his eyes widened.

Randi turned to see what he was staring at. It was Max, standing in the entrance to the living room. And she was wearing that strange black outfit, the one-piece thing that she had arrived on Earth in.

"Max!" Randi said in surprise. "What are you wearing *that* for?"

Max replied seriously. "I'm leaving, Randi. I'm going back to my own planet."

Randi's mouth fell open. She couldn't believe what she was hearing. "But, Max—why?"

Max threw up her hands helplessly. "If I can't love, I can't be human. And if I can't be human, there is no reason for me to stay here on Earth."

"But, Max, you haven't given yourself a chance!" Randi exclaimed. "You can't leave now. You have a home here—we care about you."

Max just shook her head, and Randi didn't know what to do. "Gramma!" she yelled.

Her grandmother came running out of the kitchen, wiping her hands on a dish towel. "*Now* what's the problem?"

"Max says she's leaving! She says she's going back to her own planet! Gramma, talk her out of it!"

Max just stood there stiffly. Gramma eyed her appraisingly. To Randi's surprise, she didn't look too terribly concerned. All she said was, "It's going to be dark soon, Max, and you don't want to travel at night. Have dinner, at least, and a good night's sleep. Then you can decide if you want to leave. But stick around for tonight, okay?"

Max's forehead wrinkled, and she took on an expression that Randi understood. "*Stick around* means stay for a while. Okay, Max? Will you?"

Max sighed. "It *is* a long journey. Perhaps I should wait until morning before I leave. Although the molecular transfiguration process only takes a few moments in your time, it's still exhausting."

"Good," Randi said, though she wondered if there was any chance she'd be able to change Max's mind by morning. And then, suddenly, she remembered that Gary was still standing there.

He hadn't said a word since Max entered the room. He was staring at her as if she were something from outer space—which, when Randi thought about it, was a perfectly appropriate reaction.

"Then—then it's true," he whispered. "She *is* from another planet."

"That's what I *told* you," Randi said in exasperation. "*Now* do you believe me?"

Gary looked like he was in a state of shock and didn't respond. Meanwhile, Gramma wandered over to the window and peered out. "Oh, good, here comes Bubba," she said.

"Bubba!" Randi exclaimed. "Why's he coming over?"

Her grandmother seemed completely imperturbed. "I invited him for dinner, too. I thought it would be nice to have an even number." She opened the door for him.

"Hi, guys," Bubba said. Randi smiled, and Max murmured something that sounded vaguely like a greeting. Gary didn't say a word; he was still staring at Max.

"Randi," Gary whispered, "we have to talk."

Gramma stood in the middle of the room, looking like a play director trying to figure out where to place everyone.

"Now I have to get dinner ready," she said. "Carl will be here in less than an hour. Max, Randi and Gary need to talk privately, so why don't you take Bubba down to the den."

The idea obviously pleased Bubba, but Max looked like she was only following orders. She beckoned to Bubba, and he followed her down to the den. Gramma disappeared into the kitchen.

"Gary," Randi said, "you'd better sit down. You look like you're going to pass out."

Gary obliged and fell back onto the sofa. "I can't believe it," he murmured. "She's really from outer space."

Randi sat down next to him. "That's right," she said. "Now do you understand why I've been so worried about her?"

Gary nodded slowly. "Who else knows about her?"

"Just Gramma, and Ellen," Randi replied. "Max and I made up that amnesia story. I figured most people wouldn't believe the truth. And if they did . . ." she shuddered. "I'd hate to think what would happen to Max."

"I know what you mean," Gary said. "Newspapers, television—they'd all be after her."

"I'm not even sure what to tell my parents," Randi added. "They're going to be home next week."

Gary whistled. "Wow . . . now I feel really bad for not believing you. It must be pretty weird for you, trying to help her adjust to life on Earth."

Randi nodded fervently. "No kidding. Especially because she comes from a planet where there's no emotion. Can you imagine, Gary? No friendships, no family, no . . . love."

"And now she wants to go back," Gary said. "How do you feel about that? Do you want her to stay?"

Randi nodded fervently. "Funny—when she first arrived, I couldn't wait to get rid of her. But she kind of grew on me. And now—well, I guess I always wanted a sister, and Max is the next best thing. And she's getting to act more like a human all the time. I know she belongs here. Gary, how am I going to convince her to stay?"

"I don't know," Gary said honestly. "She looked like she was pretty determined to leave."

"I know," Randi said despairingly. "And I've got to change her mind."

"You'll think of something," Gary said comfortingly. "Meanwhile, about us . . ."

"Yes?"

He looked a little abashed. "I'm sorry I didn't

believe you. I should have known you'd never lie to me."

"Never," Randi said, and she knew she meant it. "Gary—I wasn't just looking for any boyfriend. I was only looking for you."

Gary leaned over and kissed her lightly. "I love you, Randi."

Before Randi could reply, Max suddenly appeared in the room.

"Randi," she said, sounding disturbed. "I must speak with you. Will you come with me, please?"

Randi shot a bewildered look at Gary, and then followed Max upstairs. Once inside their bedroom, Max began to rummage through the closet.

"I must find something else to wear," she said in a voice higher than normal. "What I am wearing is so unattractive."

Randi stared at her. "But why are you suddenly so concerned about what you're wearing?"

Max paused and an uncertain look crossed her face. "I don't know. Bubba and I were just sitting in the den, talking, when suddenly I felt this need to change my clothes." Quickly she began undressing. "Do you think Bubba likes glitter?"

Randi was totally confused. "I don't know. What do you care what Bubba likes?"

Max looked just as confused. "I don't know! He was looking at me and I was looking at him and for some totally illogical reason, I wanted to look prettier! Why is that?"

Randi's eyes widened. "Is it because you wanted to be pretty *for* him?"

Max didn't look any less confused. "But why would I want to be pretty for him?"

" 'Cause—'cause maybe you're attracted to him!"

Max looked at her blankly, and then a look of gradual realization appeared.

"You mean—I might be in love with him?"

"Well, let's not jump to conclusions," Randi said hastily, "but something's happening—that's for sure. I don't know if it's love—but you obviously care what he thinks about you."

Max looked bewildered. "But I dated Bubba before. And I didn't care what I looked like then. Why do I care now?"

Randi grinned. "Sometimes it takes a while before you really fall for a guy."

"But what about 'love at first sight'?" Max asked, frowning. "All the books I read, the man and woman fell in love at first sight!"

"I *told* you, it doesn't always happen that way in real life," Randi replied. "Only in books."

"You mean," Max said slowly, wonderingly, "that this strange sensation . . . it might be love?"

"It might be," Randi said cautiously. "It's hard to say."

Max stood very still. And then, slowly, as if in slow motion, she began to change her clothes.

"I *am* enjoying his company," she said thoughtfully.

"That's good," Randi said encouragingly.

"And there's something about him that I did not notice before."

"What's that?" Randi asked.

"I'm not sure," Max admitted. "I guess I'm going to have to spend a lot more time with him so that I can figure out what it is."

"That sounds like the beginning of a relationship," Randi said enthusiastically.

Max examined herself in the mirror and looked at the reflection of Randi behind her.

"But is it love?"

Randi shrugged. "I don't know. Maybe it is, and maybe it isn't. I guess you'll figure it out eventually. Or maybe you won't."

Max sighed. "Earth is a very strange place. No definitions, no explanations. Nothing makes any sense at all. It's unpredictable and illogical."

"That's true," Randi admitted.

Max turned away from the mirror, facing Randi directly. And then she began to smile.

"But interesting," she said. "Definitely interesting. And I think . . . I think . . ."

"What?"

Her smile widened.

"I think I'll stick around."

*Other books in this series*

## MAX ON EARTH
### Marilyn Kaye

The first book about strange, golden-haired Max, the alien being from another world, in which she comes to Earth to learn how to behave in a human manner and picks on Randi Hill as the person to help her. She learns quickly and makes friends – but when it comes to understanding human emotions, poor Max is at a loss.

## THE FORTUNATE FEW
### – Tim Kennemore

Jodie Bell is a professional gymnast – starved to the perfect weight, worked to the point of collapse and sold to the highest bidder. A thought-provoking story, set in the not too distant future.

## AN OPEN MIND
### Susan Sallis

A subtle and compassionate teenage novel in which David, working as a volunteer at a spastic school, gradually comes to terms with his parents' divorce and its effect on his life.

## THE DAY THEY CAME
## TO ARREST THE BOOK
*Nat Hentoff*

When an attempt is made to ban *Huckleberry Finn* from an American school because of alleged racism, the ensuing row rapidly involves not only the pupils and their teachers but the whole community as well.

## THE BEST LITTLE GIRL
## IN THE WORLD
*Steven Levenkron*

Francesca had never given her parents any worry, until her ambitions to become a ballet dancer result in anorexia. A compelling story.

## HEY, DIDI DARLING
*S. A. Kennedy*

A highly entertaining and amusing story which follows a rock group's progress from its first high school dance to the finals of a music contest.

## CLOUDY / BRIGHT
### John Rowe Townsend

A sensitive and amusing contemporary love story about two young aspiring photographers.

## ROLL OF THUNDER, HEAR MY CRY
### Mildred D. Taylor

Set in the Mississippi of 1930, the story of one black family's struggle to keep their independence against the oppression of a cruelly racist society.

## OF GRIFFINS AND GRAFFITI
### Kate Gilmore

Exciting story of a group of New York teenagers with a passion for graffiti – the often beautiful wall paintings, not the mindless, illiterate scrawls – who long to pull off a really big 'piece'.